THE HIDDEN TREASURES
OF THE CHRISTIAN FAITH

Pastor Midagbodji Ablam (Abraham)

Kingdom
Publishers

The Hidden Treasures of the Christian Faith
Copyright © Abraham Midagbodji Ablam

All rights reserved. No part of this book may be reproduced in any form by photocopying or any electronic or mechanical means, including information storage or retrieval systems, without permission in writing from both the copyright owner and the publisher of the book. The right of John Lloyd to be identified as the author of this work has been asserted by him in accordance with the Copyright, Designs and Patents Act 1988 and any subsequent amendments thereto. A catalogue record for this book is available from the British Library. All scripture quotations unless otherwise stated are taken from the Kings James Version of the Bible.

ISBN: 978-1-913247-05-8

1st Edition by Kingdom Publishers
Kingdom Publishers
London, UK.

The Table of Contents

INTRODUCTION — 11

Chapter One
- The Three Churches on Earth — 17

Chapter Two
- Faith and Understanding — 34

Chapter Three
- Power and Revelation — 39

Chapter Four
- The Mysteries of the Christian Faith — 43

Chapter Five
- The Manifestation of the Eternal Life — 46

Chapter Six
- The True God and the Eternal Life — 53

Chapter Seven
- The Church of Jesus Christ is married to Jesus Christ — 58

Chapter Eight
- Preaching another Jesus, another Spirit and another Gospel — 62

Chapter Nine
- The good Wine and the wine of the Woman's fornication — 66

Chapter Ten
- There are Three that bears record in Heaven and on Earth — 75

Chapter Eleven
- The Spirit of Truth and the spirit of Error — 79

Chapter Twelve
- The Mystery of the Rapture and the Resurrection — 85

Chapter Thirteen
- Faithfulness in stewardship — 89

DEDICATION

This book is dedicated to the Almighty God who came into this world in the form of MAN (Jesus Christ) to die, saving the whole world through His Death, Burial and Resurrection.

Secondly, I dedicate it to the apostolic fathers of the early Church who were killed by the enemies of TRUTH, but whose **PATH** could still be traced from the Bible by the seekers of the apostolic TRUTH.

Finally, I dedicate it to the hungry and thirsty souls in the Church of Jesus Christ, who are still breaking the fallow apostolic grounds (Foundation) in search of the hidden apostolic TRUTH.

ACKNOWLEDGEMENTS

I thank my Creator and Savior Jesus Christ, whose mercy and compassion have elected me and graced me with the revelation of end time revival "apostolic mysteries" that have been covered for years. I thank my wife, children and the members of the **Holy Faith Pentecostal Church** in Udine, Italy, Lomé and Togo, whose efforts, both spiritual and physical have helped me realize the vision of this Book.

Thanks to my Pastor, district elder John Gyasi whose initiative is the seed that has eventually blossomed into the bearing of this fruit.

Finally, my appreciation goes to the prayer Pillars and prayer Warriors who stand in the gap by praying and interceding for the Body of Christ worldwide.

INTRODUCTION

— *He made known his ways unto Moses, his acts unto the children of Israel. (Ps 103:7, KJV)*

— *He answered and said unto them, because it is given unto you to know the mysteries of kingdom of heaven, but to them it is not given. For whosoever hath, to him shall be given, and he shall have more abundance; but whosoever hath not, from him shall be taken away even that he hath. Therefore, speak I to them in parables: because seeing they see not; and hearing they hear not, neither do they understand. And in them is fulfilled the prophecy of Esaias, which saith, by hearing ye shall hear, and shall not understand; and seeing ye shall see, and shall not perceive. (Matt 13:11-14, KJV)*

— *Again, the kingdom of heaven is like unto treasure hid in a field; the which when a man hath found, he hideth, and for joy thereof goeth and selleth all that he hath, and buyeth that field. (Matt 13:44, KJV) --- Let a man so account of us, as of the ministers of Christ, and stewards of the mysteries of God. Moreover, it is required in stewards, that a man be found faithful. (1 Corin 4:1-2, KJV)*

The mysteries of God are His eternal plan that has been revealed unto His chosen people, the elect by His grace through His Spirit, while to others it remains in parables according to the word of God. This statement from our Lord and Savior Jesus Christ is enough to silence every unnecessary argument within Christendom. If it is given to some (the elect) to understand the mysteries of the kingdom while to others it is not given, this means it remains in parables, the conclusion we draw is that are two groups of Christians in the kingdom who cannot agree and work together because one party is holding unto the parables, while the other party is given the understanding to unveil the mysteries of the kingdom of heaven.

After His resurrection, the Lord opened the understanding of His disciples (the chosen ones) to understand the scriptures, because as Jews they were affected by the prophecy of Isaiah that says, *"Seeing they shall see but shall not perceive and hearing they shall hear but shall not understand"*. Thus, it is important that every Jew has his eyes and understanding open to comprehend and grasp what Jesus Christ came to do in this world. The PERSECUTORS of the apostolic TRUTH had been of old and will continue to persecute the ELECT till the Lord returns for His children. The people, the Jews, to whom the TRUTH was sent during the days of Apostle Paul rejected it by telling the Apostle to tell them his thoughts and not the TRUTH, because the truth of the apostolic message was being antagonized everywhere it was preached. Now let's see from the scriptures how Apostle Paul ended with his brethren concerning this matter:

— And when they had appointed him a day, there came many to him into his lodging; to whom he expounded and testified the kingdom of God, persuading them concerning Jesus, both out of the law of Moses, and out of the prophets, from morning till evening. And some believed the things which were spoken, and some believed not. And when they agreed not among themselves, they departed, after that Paul had spoken one word, Well spake the Holy Ghost by Esaias the prophet unto our fathers, Saying, Go unto this people, and say, Hearing ye shall hear, and shall not understand; and seeing ye shall see, and not perceive:

For the heart of this people is waxed gross, and their ears are dull of hearing, and their eyes have they closed; lest they should see with their eyes, and hear with their ears, and understand with their heart, and should be converted, and I should heal them. Be it known therefore unto you, that the salvation of God is sent unto the Gentiles, and that they will hear it. And when he had said these words, the Jews departed, and had great reasoning among themselves. And Paul dwelt two whole years in his own hired house, and received all that came in unto him, Preaching the kingdom of God, and teaching those things which concern the Lord Jesus Christ, with all confidence, no man forbidden him. (Acts 28:23-31, KJV)

After the resurrection, the Lord Jesus Christ did two things to His followers, He opened their eyes to see Him and He opened their understanding to understand the scriptures from the Law of Moses, from the Psalms and from the Prophets. Then, He sent them away few days after pouring His Spirit upon them for witnessing. See the following scriptures:

— And he said unto them, These are the words which I spake unto you, while I was yet with you, that all things must be fulfilled, which were written in the law of Moses, and in the prophets, and in the psalms, concerning me. Then opened he their understanding, that they might understand the scriptures, And said unto them, Thus it is written, and thus it behooved Christ to suffer, and to rise from the dead the third day: And that repentance and remission of sins should be preached in his name among all nations, beginning at Jerusalem. And ye are witnesses of these things. And, behold, I send the promise of my Father upon you: but tarry ye in the city of Jerusalem, until ye be endued with power from on high. (Luke 24:44-49, KJV)

We can now see from the scriptures that the Lord did these two things unto His disciples to wipe out confusion from them. First, He opened their understanding to understand the scriptures, so when the Bible says *"for lack of knowledge my people perish and lack of knowledge they have gone into captivity"* there is no doubt about that because the word of God is TRUE.

Those who are holding unto the parables (the physical understanding of the Word) of the WORD, and the mysteries (the spiritual understanding of the WORD) cannot stay together so they will persecute each other unless they live in compromise or they humbly agree to study the WORD of God together in search of the TRUTH. It is written that: ---- *But as then he that was born after the flesh persecuted him that was born after the Spirit, even so it is now. (Gal. 4:29)*

People who followed Jesus Christ for physical bread soon stopped following Him, when it came to spiritual bread which entailed eating of His flesh and the drinking of His blood, the Lord said many are called but few are chosen. After the Lord spoke about the BREAD OF LIFE, His followers left him one after another until it remained only His disciples whom he asked, will you also go away?

Peter answered the Lord saying, "to whom shall we go? For you are the one who has the words of eternal life". Only the chosen ones can follow Jesus Christ to the end if spiritual truths are being preached or taught in His Church. The Bible says: *"God by wisdom has founded the world, but by understanding has He established it"*. It is

evident from this scripture that God founded His Church by wisdom who is Jesus Christ, and established it by understanding. Understanding the mysteries of the kingdom of God can only come by revelation from God, that is why the last thing the Lord did unto His Apostles before leaving them to Heaven was to open their understanding to comprehend the scriptures. When He ascended into His glory, He revealed the last mystery which was hidden in the book of Daniel through the last of the twelve Apostles, Apostle John, who authored the Book of Revelation. In this Book, John revealed the past, the present, the future and who Jesus is. That means every hidden mystery has been revealed through God's chosen people, but what we need now is understanding. Jesus Christ used Apostle Paul as the vessel through which He revealed many things that were hidden from the Jews.

When we read the Bible through the lens of our carnal imaginations, we create our own revelations and misinterpret the truth of the Word of God, this leads to confusion, and engenders hatred and contention among the brethren.

I ask you to humbly go unto the Lord in prayer and ask for His mercy and compassion so that you can be led into deeper understanding. As you continue reading this book, I trust that your understanding will be deepened when reading/teaching the word of God.

Apostle Paul has made the matter clear to us when he said we know in part. Our problem today as the ministers of God is the misappropriation of gifts; if somebody has the gift of healing and then interprets the whole Bible through the lens of that gift, it leads to accidents within the body, dead bodies are carried for burial, because he goes out from his rail and crash with another man who is on his track. If you discover that there are some scriptures which you have boldly preached and taught wrongly, don't allow pride to harden your heart, humbly go to the Lord in prayer for amendment and restoration, because it is written that:

— Even him, whose coming is after the working of Satan with all power and signs and lying wonders, and with all deceivableness of unrighteousness in them that perish; because they received not the love of the truth, that they might be saved. And for this cause God shall send them strong delusion, that they should believe a lie: That they all might be damned who believed not the truth, but had pleasure in unrighteousness. (2 Thess. 2:9-12)

Take heed, brethren, lest there be in any of you an evil heart of unbelief, in departing from the living God. But exhort one another daily, while it is called Today; lest any of you be hardened through the deceitfulness of sin. For we are made partakers of Christ, if we hold the beginning of our confidence steadfast unto the end; While it is said, today if ye will hear his voice, harden not your hearts, as in the provocation. (Heb. 3:12-15)

Many people have been deceived to believe that theology is part of Christianity, so they spend most of their time and money in the school of theology. According to the Oxford advanced learner's dictionary for international students, theology is explained as the study of religion and beliefs. There is nothing wrong about the study of theology if it is for personal knowledge but it is wrong to search for the invisible God in the field of theology, because the all-knowing God chose Apostle Paul who was well learned in his time, and revealed the mysteries of the Kingdom to him and made him the leader and the teacher of the Gentiles. He did this to silence the voice of the theologians from His Church. If Apostle Paul who was well learned in his time could not know the mysteries of CHRIST till it was revealed onto him, then how many theologians in our time in the Church are deceiving themselves and their followers? Mysteries are understood by revelations, while the study of theology gives knowledge and experience.

— *Stay yourselves, and wonder; cry ye out, and cry: they are drunken, but not with wine; they stagger, but not with strong drink. For the LORD hath poured out upon you the spirit of deep sleep, and hath closed your eyes: the prophets and your rulers, the seers hath he covered. And the vision of all is become unto you as the words of a book that is sealed, which men deliver to one that is learned, saying, Read this, I pray thee: and he saith, I cannot: for it is sealed: And the book is delivered to him that is not learned, saying, Read this, I pray thee: and he saith, I am not learned. (Is 29:9-12)*

Summarily, the mysteries of the Kingdom of God are understood by revelations according to God's given gifts, while the study of theology gives knowledge and experience about religion. As a matter of fact, seeking the Jewish God-the God of Abraham, Isaac and Jacob with the Gentile mentality is the cause of increasing idolatry in the Christian FAITH. This is where the Romans got it wrong and distributed to the world, the WINE of their FORNICATION which is the belief in TRINITY, with explanations of GOD IN THREE PERSONS-BLESSED TRINITY. The One true God of the Jews never introduced Himself to any of His chosen Prophets as more than ONE God, ONE LORD, ONE Creator and ONE Savior in spite of His many works that added crowned Him with many titles apart from His ONE NAME JEHOVAH. His servant Moses told the Jews that: *Hear, O Israel: The LORD our God is one LORD: And thou shalt love the LORD thy God with all thy heart, and with all thy soul, and withal thy might. And these words, which I command thee this day, shall be in thine heart.* I urge you to humbly read on and I pray the Lord gives you the light of understanding Him the more. Amen!

CHAPTER ONE

THE THREE CHURCHES ON EARTH

Again, the kingdom of heaven is like unto a net, that was cast into the sea, and gathered of every kind: Which, when it was full, they drew to shore, and sat down, and gathered the good into vessels, but cast the bad away. So, shall it be at the end of the world: the angels shall come forth, and sever the wicked from among the just, and shall cast them into the furnace of fire: there shall be wailing and gnashing of teeth. Jesus saith unto them, have ye understood all these things? They say unto him, Yea, Lord. (Matt 13:47-51)

Although there are millions of churches on this earth, some of whose roots we can trace and some we can't, especially the occultist churches. If we search for the True Church of Jesus Christ using the Bible as our guide, we can easily come out from the hands of the enemy who is leading many people with his deception into destruction. If we trace the foundation of our churches from the Bible, it will help us to know if we are worshiping man, the devil or our Lord and Saviour Jesus Christ. Jesus said **"I am the Light of the World, he who walks in me shall never walk in darkness"** The devil and his cohorts have entered into the ministry by setting up churches as an avenue to lead people to destruction why they think they are worshiping the True God of the Jews —Jehovah who came in the form of a man as Jesus Christ of Nazareth. Apostle Paul warned Timothy, his son in the Lord, to take heed unto himself and unto the DOCTRINE and by so doing he would save himself and those who would hear and follow him.

The truth about this deception is that, there are THREE CHURCHES on this earth and each one of them has a DOCTRINE. All these churches are functioning very well with each and every one of them claiming that they are the CHOSEN CHURCH by

Jesus Christ. These three churches can be traced from the scriptures through the DOCTRINE each one of them preach and teach. They are as follows –

1. **The church of man who teaches and preaches the Doctrine (the mind) of man, by quoting from the Bible.**

2. **The Church of God-Jesus Christ who teaches and preaches the Doctrine (the mind) of Christ, by quoting from the Bible.**

3. **The church of Satan (BABYLON THE GREAT, THE MOTHER OF HARLOTS AND ABOMINATIONS OF THE EARTH) who teaches and preaches the Doctrine (mind) of devils, by quoting from the Bible.**

THE THREE CHURCHES

This is the main reason why the churches cannot come together as a unified church. All these announcements of global leadership everywhere that involves the Christians, other religions and unbelievers together in **LEADERSHIP TRAINING** is nothing more than training and preparing the people for the soon coming antichrist, it doesn't matter how nicely and successfully the whole meeting may be in the end. If the Apostles of Jesus Christ could be here today to see people who calls themselves apostles mingling with people of different **RELIGIOUS FAITHS**, they would regret their suffering. The true APOSTOLICS who understood what it meant to be disciples of Jesus Christ and apostolic leaders would not be found in any gathering where every DOCTRINE is accepted, and that was the starting point of their persecution.

Let us trace the THREE CHURCHES from the scriptures so that we can know our position in this religious and confused world. We must bear in mind that the God of Abraham, Isaac and Jacob, Jehovah of the Jews has two types of people here on earth, the physical Jews-Israelites and the spiritual Jews, the Church of Jesus Christ also known as the born-again Christians from the Gentile world or the other nations. They are as follows —

1. **THE CHURCH IN THE WILDERNESS (THE JEWS ONLY)**

— This is that Moses, which said unto the children of Israel, A prophet shall the Lord your God raise up unto you of your brethren, like unto me; him shall ye hear. This is he, that was in the church in the wilderness with the angel which spake to him in mount Sinai, and with our fathers: who received the lively oracles to give unto us: To whom our fathers would not obey, but thrust him from them, and in their hearts turned back again into Egypt (Acts 7:37-39)

In the Church in the Wilderness, God – the One True Jehovah of the Hebrews dealt only with the physical children of Abraham known as the Jews. He gave them a leader and a teacher called Moses to whom He gave His laws and ways (Doctrine) and through whom He taught His people. So, the Bible says --- **He made known his ways unto Moses, his acts unto the children of Israel. (Ps 103:7),** when God walked among His people by showing them His acts, He added more titles to His one Name Jehovah. To warn His children not to be deceived by the worshipers of other gods, He gave them the doctrine of oneness, which means in all His different manifestations they should not think that He is more than one God (Jehovah).

— Hear therefore, O Israel, and observe to do it; that it may be well with thee, and that ye may increase mightily, as the LORD God of thy fathers hath promised thee, in the land that floweth with milk and honey. Hear, O Israel: The LORD our God is one LORD: And thou shalt love the LORD thy God with all thine heart, and with all thy soul, and with all thy might. And these words, which I command thee this day,

shall be in thine heart. (Deut 6:3-6)

The God of Abraham, Isaac and Jacob was known unto the Jews as Jehovah and He did a lot of miracles in their midst which created for Him many **TITLES,** but He warned His people never to think that as their God, He is more than One Jehovah. When He manifested Himself in the flesh as Jesus Christ, He was also tested by the scribes with that scripture which was earlier given unto them as their greatest DOCTRINE and commandment.

— And one of the scribes came, and having heard them reasoning together, and perceiving that he had answered them well, asked him, which is the first commandment of all? And Jesus answered him, The first of all the commandments is, Hear, O Israel; The Lord our God is one Lord: And thou shalt love the Lord thy God with all thy heart, and with all thy soul, and with all thy mind, and with all thy strength: this is the first commandment. And the second is like, namely this, Thou shalt love thy neighbour as thyself. There is none other commandment greater than these. And the scribe said unto him, Well Master, thou hast said the truth: for there is one God; and there is none other but he. And to love him with all the heart, and with all the understanding, and with all the soul, and with all the strength, and to love his neighbour as himself, is more than all whole burnt offerings and sacrifices. And when Jesus saw that he answered discreetly, he said unto him, Thou art not far from the kingdom of God. And no man after that durst ask him any question. (Mark 12:28-34)

It is clearly written on the pages of the scriptures that God is not an author of confusion, so if we want to walk with this God, we must be ready to humble ourselves in obedience and follow His instructions that always lead to life, peace and blessings. The primary criteria for entrance into the Church in the wilderness was by physical **CIRCUMCISION**. The Church in the wilderness was led by Moses, after his death his minister Joshua continued till they reached the Promised Land. This was a typology of the new things the Lord promised to do in saving the whole world; The Bible says: -- *- For the law was given by Moses, but grace and truth came by Jesus Christ. (John 1:17)* It is important that Christians fully understand the pattern of the Church in the wilderness as it would help end all needless arguments with false churches and their leaders who have been employed by the devil and his demons to create confusion in

Christendom. To deepen your understanding, with open heart, study the following drawing that teaches about the FOUNDATIONS of these two Jewish nations (the physical Israelites and the spiritual Israelites who are the born again Christians from the other nations.)

THE BUILDING PLAN OF THE TWO JEWISH NATIONS – PHYSICAL AND SPIRITUAL

2. THE CHURCH IN JERUSALEM-THE CITY OF DAVID (THE CHRISTIANS WORLDWILDE)

The Church in Jerusalem refers to the spiritual children of Abraham, whose God is the God of Abraham, Isaac and Jacob. Jesus Christ is the Jehovah of the Jews who manifested Himself in the flesh to save the children of Adam and Eve who are flesh and blood. A lot of Bible scholars question why the Lord gave the KEYS to the kingdom to Apostle Peter and not John the beloved. For the Lord Jesus Christ, to build His Church in this confused and religious world where Satan and his demons are also looking for souls to draft into hell, one of His chosen Apostles must answer the prophetic question of Isaiah the Prophet o as to qualify as the key holders of the Kingdom of Heaven.

— *Who hath believed our report? And to whom is the arm of the LORD revealed? (Is 53:1)*

— When Jesus came into the coasts of Caesarea Philippi, he asked his disciples, saying, Whom do men say that I the Son of man am? And they said, some say that thou art John the Baptist: some, Elias; and others, Jeremias, or one of the prophets. He saith unto them, but Whom say ye that I am? And Simon Peter answered and said, Thou art the Christ, the Son of the living God. And Jesus answered and said unto him, Blessed art thou, Simon Bar-jona: for flesh and blood hath not revealed it unto thee, but my Father which is in heaven. And I say also unto thee, Thou art Peter, and upon this rock I will build my church; and the gates of hell shall not prevail against it. And I will give unto thee the keys of the kingdom of heaven: and whatsoever thou shalt bind on earth shall be bound in heaven: and whatsoever thou shalt loose on earth shall be loosed in heaven. (Matt 16:13-19)

If we compare the above scriptures, we could see that Apostle Peter answered the prophetic question which Isaiah the Prophet asked when he said --**to whom the ARM of the Lord is revealed?** The whole chapter of Isaiah 53 talks about the CHURCH and the rejected Messiah by whose stripes we are healed. The Lord commanded His disciples to wait at Jerusalem for the Holy Ghost and start His Church from there so that any false church that uses His Name could be detected through their teachings (**DOCTRINES**). The Church in the wilderness i.e.the Jews holds unto the physical circumcision according to the Law and believe in seeing miracles with their naked eyes. The Church in Jerusalem i.e. the spiritual Jews holds unto the spiritual circumcision which is baptism in Jesus' name for the remission of sins and they walk by faith and grace and not by sight. Both churches belong to the one true God of Abraham, Isaac and Jacob who was in the midst of the Jews as Jehovah but manifested Himself in the flesh as the Son of God to build His Church. In this Church (the Church of Jesus Christ), to the principal thing is to understand that Jesus Christ was crucified on the CROSS for man's salvation, Jesus was the one crucified and not any church or any denominational leader, so all the glory in His Church must be given onto Him and no one else.

GET THE UNDERSTANDING:*Read the following scriptures meditatively as you trace how God built the Nation of Israel with the twelve sons (tribes) of Jacob-Israel and the Church of Jesus Christ, the spiritual Israelites with the twelve Apostles.*

Hearken to me, ye that follow after righteousness, ye that seek the LORD: look unto the rock whence ye are hewn, and to the hole of the pit whence ye are digged. Look unto Abraham your father, and unto Sarah that bare you: for I called him alone, and blessed him, and increased him. For the LORD shall comfort Zion: he will comfort all her waste places; and he will make her wilderness like Eden and her desert like the garden of the LORD; joy and gladness shall be found therein, thanksgiving, and the voice of melody. Hearken unto me, my people; and give ear unto me, O my nation: for a law shall proceed from me, and I will make my judgment to rest for a light of the people. (Isa 51:1-2) If we study the above pictures of the two Jewish Nations very well, we could see that God is not an author of confusion, so He does His things to help mortal men understand Him and know His ways so they can follow Him with full conviction and not be deceived by the Devil and his kingdom workers. In building the Jewish nation, God chose the seed of Isaac Abraham's son called Jacob by his father and changed his name to Israel. Out of His chosen one-Jacob now known as Israel came forth the twelve sons known as the twelve tribes (Pillars) of Israel. It is evidently written in the scriptures that: **Blessed is the nation whose God is the Lord; and the people whom he hath chosen for his own inheritance. The Lord looketh from heaven; he beholdeth all the sons of men. From the place of his habitation he looketh upon all the inhabitants of the earth. Ps 33:12-14**

But thou, Israel, art my servant, Jacob whom I have chosen, the seed of Abraham my friend. Thou whom I have taken from the ends of the earth, and called thee from the chief men thereof, and said unto thee. Thou art my servant, I have chosen thee, and not cast thee away. Is 41:8-9.

God set Israel aside as a clear picture of His future Church which He later came to build through His twelve Apostles in the New Testament. A careful study of the scriptures would reveal that God laid Abraham as the foundation of many nations through whom the Jewish nation came forth, by a promised son called Isaac. Isaac in turn gave birth to Esau and Jacob, twins (two nations) among whom God chose one who is Jacob and changed his name to Israel and built His nation through him. Genesis chapter 25 has the story. Although many nations came out of Abraham, but not all of them are Jews, or chosen by God. **Behold I will make them of the synagogue of Satan, which say they are Jews, and are not, but do lie, behold, I will make them to come and worship before thy feet and to know that I have loved thee. Rev 3:9.** In this Church dispensation, not everyone who calls himself or herself a Christian or a child of Abraham is acknowledged by God, only the elect. To the elect it is given to understand the mysteries of the Kingdom of God, but to others it shall remain a mystery. God is a Master builder who plans before doing anything. So it is written that:

And after they had held their peace, James answered, saying, Men and brethren, hearken unto me: Simeon hath declared how God at the first did visit the Gentiles, to take out of them a people for his name. And to this agree the words of the prophets; as it is written. After this I will return, and will build again the tabernacle of David, which was fallen down; and I will build again the ruins thereof, and I will set it up. That the residue of men might seek after the Lord, and all the Gentiles, upon whom my name is called, saith the Lord, who doeth all these things. Known unto God are all his works from the beginning of the world. Acts 15:13-18

THE OLD AND NEW JERUSALEM

The nation of Israel and the city of Jerusalem is set apart as an example for God's elect on this Earth. A careful study on it would help Christians know and understand if we are part of God's people for whom the New Jerusalem is prepared or not. The Bible speaks about the TWENTY FOUR ELDERS in the Book of Revelation, who we understand comprise the twelve Apostles who stands as the twelve Pillars of the New Testament Church of Jesus Christ and the twelve sons-tribes of Jacob who formed the nation of Israel.

If we follow God's WORD, we will be saved, but if we follow our own imaginations while we neglect the leadership of the Holy Ghost who is the glorious representative of Christ in us, and the WORD of God, we will end up blaming ourselves and not even the devil. The scriptures are given for our direction in connection with God's Spirit, so that if the devil and his ministers disguise themselves as ministers of light we may discern their lies through the WORD and the Spirit of God. Let see from the scriptures how God divided the Promised Land where this present Jerusalem could be found, to His people the Jews.

This is the land which ye shall divide by lot unto the tribes of Israel for inheritance, and these are their portions, saith the Lord GOD. And these are the

goings out of the city on the north side, four thousand and five hundred measures. And the gates of the city shall be after the names of the tribes of Israel: three gates northward; one gate of Reuben, one gate of Judah, one gate of Levi. And at east side four thousand and five hundred: and three gates; and one gate of Joseph, one gate of Benjamin, one gate of Dan. And at the south side four thousand and five hundred measures: and three gates; one gate of Simeon, one gate of Issachar, one gate of Zebulun. At the west side four thousand and five hundred, with their gates; one gate of Gad, one gate of Asher, one gate of Naphtali. It was round about eighteen thousand measures: and the name of the city from that day shall be, The Lord is there. Ezekiel 48:29-35

And he carried me away in the spirit to a great and high mountain, and showed me that great city, the holy Jerusalem, descending out of heaven from God, Having the glory of God: and her light was like unto a stone most precious, even like a jasper stone, clear as crystal; And had a wall great and high, and had twelve gates, and at the gates twelve angels, and names written thereon, which are the names of the twelve tribes of the children of Israel: On the east three gates; on the north three gates; on the south three gates; and on the west three gates. And the wall of the city had twelve foundations, and in them the names of the twelve apostles of the Lamb. And the city lieth four-square, and the length is as large as the breath: and he measured the city with the reed, twelve thousand furlongs. The length and the breadth and the height of it are equal. Rev 21:10-14

If the physical Jews know their ROOT, then what should we say about the spiritual Jews who are born again and worship God by faith? If we want to trace our root as spiritual Jews-God chosen Church among the Churches, then we must search the scriptures and not to be followers of men. As Gentiles, we became the children of Abraham through the BORN AGAIN process facilitated by the apostles' DOCTRINES of BAPTISM-born again of water and of the Spirit. It is part of the blood covenant that God made with man in saving him from the wrath of God that is coming soon upon the whole world.

For ye are all the children of God by faith in Christ Jesus. For as many of you as have been baptized into Christ have put on Christ. There is neither bond nor free, there is neither male nor female: for ye are all one in Christ Jesus. And if ye be Christ's, then are ye Abraham's seed, and heirs according to the promise. Gal 3:26-29

But now in Christ Jesus ye who sometimes were far off are made nigh by the blood of Christ. For he is our peace, who hath made both one, and hath broken down the middle wall of partition between us; Having abolished in his flesh the enmity, even the law of commandments contained in ordinances; for to make in himself of twain one new man, so making peace; And that he might reconcile both unto God in one body by the cross, having slain the enmity thereby: And came and preached peace to you which were afar off, and to them that were nigh. For through him we both have access by one Spirit unto the Father. Now therefore ye are no more strangers and foreigners, but fellow citizens with the saints, and of the household of God; And are built upon the foundation of the apostles and prophets, Jesus Christ hImself being the chief corner stone; In whom all the building fitly framed together growth unto an holy temple in the Lord: In whom ye also are builded together for an habitation of God through the Spirit. Eph 2:13-22.

The conclusion about the CHRISTIAN race is that it is not hidden from the people of God, rather our own imaginations are leading us from the Lord into idolatry. The true children of God are not saved by miracles, healing, signs and wonders, but by the revelation of the mystery of the CROSS of Calvary on which Jesus Christ-the Lamb of God was crucified, shedding His BLOOD. Let God be TRUE and let every man be a liar. The salvation of the souls of humanity is a MYSTERY hidden in the BLOOD COVENANT which God made with man after he sinned in the Garden of Eden. When Adam and Eve disobeyed God, there was no priest to sacrifice animal to atone for their sins, so God Himself became the PRIEST, and sacrificed-shed the blood of an animal for their COVERING. The MYSTERY of the BLOOD COVENANT is still hidden from many who claim they have been called by God to do His work, that is why people are no more preaching about the CROSS. To the Jewish nation it is the blood-souls of their fathers through the circumcision that speaks to God as a covenant right that, **"we-the Jews belongs to You".** But, for both the Jews and the elect Gentiles, it is the BLOOD-SOUL of God which He shed through His Son-the Christ that speaks as a COVENANT right of sons-hip for our salvation. The Bible says:

For I would not, brethren, that ye should be ignorant of this mystery, lest ye should be wise in your own conceits; that blindness in part is happened to Israel,

until the fullness of the Gentiles be come in. And so all Israel shall be saved: as it is written. There shall come out of Zion the Deliverer, and shall turn away ungodliness from Jacob: For this is my covenant unto them, when I shall take away their sins. As concerning the gospel, they are enemies for your sakes: but as touching the election, they are beloved for the fathers' sakes. For the gifts and calling of God are without repentance. For as ye in times past have not believed God, yet have now obtained mercy through their unbelief: Even so have these also now not believed, that through your mercy they also may obtain mercy. For God hath concluded them all in unbelief, that he might have mercy upon all. Rom 11:25-32

It is written in the scriptures that: Many in the congregation are called but few i.e. the elect are chosen. In much the same way, God's works of salvation for the souls of humanity always come attached with warnings and punishments stemming from disobedience caused by the deceit of the Old Serpent known as Satan and the devil. God has spoken expressly to anyone who claims Christianity, to look unto Abraham the founding father of faith, because He called him alone and blessed him. The Church today has forgotten entirely that Jews are not the only children of Abraham, there are other people who came through his bloodline but are known as other nations. Likewise, today in the Church many claim that they are the children of Abraham without tracing their root to know if they are among the chosen-saved or the cast out.

Therefore, we ought to give the more earnest heed to the things which we have heard, lest at any time we should let them slip. For the word spoken by angels was steadfast, and every transgression and disobedience received a just recompence of reward; How shall we escape, if we neglect so great salvation; which at first began to be spoken by the Lord, and was confirmed unto us by them that heard him; God also bearing them witness, both with signs and wonders, and with divers miracles, and gifts of the Holy Ghost, according to his own will? Heb 2:1-4

This scripture concludes this whole matter and sums up the sufferings of our Lord and Savior Jesus Christ and His Apostles, what is written down for those who wants to be saved from the LAKE of FIRE, so that we can run the Christian race on the rightful TRACK with understanding in search for the salvation of our souls.

2. THE CHURCH OF MAN AND THE DOCTRINES (MIND) OF MAN

A lot of men that have built churches here on earth use the Bible and preach Jesus Christ but they are not led by the Spirit of Jesus Christ. Most of these people are well learned and graduates from different universities and Bible colleges, who use theology and their own ideologies to lead the members of their churches. These sort of leaders pride themselves in their physical knowledge of the Word of God, and those who are not led by the Spirit of Jesus Christ call such deceivers anointed men of God. You can't change them and even if you teach them the TRUTH from the Bible, they will not accept it, so the best way to deal with them is to separate yourself from them.

Apostle Paul met those sorts of people during his ministry in the school of one Tyrannus in Ephesus. And because he couldn't change the whole school he separated his converts or the disciples from them while he disputed with them and persuaded them daily for the period of two years. Let us read from the following scriptures for the confirmation. --- *And he went into the synagogue, and spake boldly for the space of three months, disputing and persuading the things concerning the kingdom of God. But when divers were hardened, and believed not, but spake evil of that way before the multitude, he departed from them, and separated the disciples, disputing daily in the school of one Tyrannus. And this continued by the space of two years; so that all they which dwelt in Asia heard the word of the Lord Jesus, both Jews and Greeks. (Acts 19:8-10)*

— Salute one another with an holy kiss. The churches of Christ salute you. Now I beseech you, brethren, mark them which cause divisions and offences contrary to the doctrine which ye have learned: and avoid them. For they that are such serve not our Lord Jesus Christ, but their own belly; and by good words and fair speeches deceive the hearts of the simple. (Romans 16:16-18)

Brethren, be followers together of me, and mark them which walk so as ye have us for an example. (For many walk, of whom I have told you often, and now tell you even weeping, that they are the enemies of the cross of

Christ: Whose end is destruction, whose God is their belly, and whose glory is in their shame, who mind earthly things.) For our conversation is in heaven; from whence also we look for the Saviour, the Lord Jesus Christ. (Phil 3:17-20)

The above scriptures prove that many men build churches for their personal gain in this world. This is the main reason why SALVATION is not being preached any more in many churches. In those types of churches, any time they call for revival they don't teach salvation, deliverance and holiness. What they do during revival meeting is to bring in another Pastor from their group who would come and with sweet words collect money from the people. Since they don't have the mind of Christ, but the mind of the god of this world they talk more about the things of this world than the things of heaven. To be frank, prosperity and blessings in every area of the Christian's life, is God's pleasure so we can't do away with them and still move forward in the Lord, but what blocks the goodness of God in the life of God's people is sin that is why we must deal with them seriously, and blessings and prosperity will come by itself.

3. THE CHURCH OF SATAN AND THE DOCTRINES OF DEVILS

— And there came one of the seven angles which had the seven vials, and talked with me, saying unto me, Come hither; I will shew unto thee the judgment of the great whore that sitteth upon many waters: With whom the kings of the earth have committed fornication, and the inhabitants of the earth have been made drunk with the wine of her fornication. So he carried me away in the spirit into the wilderness: and I saw a woman sit upon a scarlet coloured beast, full of names of blasphemy, having seven heads and ten horns. And the woman was arrayed in purple and scarlet colour, and decked with gold and precious stones and pearls, having a golden cup in her hand full of abominations and filthiness of her fornication: And upon her forehead was a name written, MYSTERY, BABYLON THE GREAT, THE MOTHER OF HARLOTS AND ABOMINATIONS OF THE EARRTH. And I saw the woman drunken with the blood of the saints, and with the blood of the martyrs of Jesus: and when I saw her, I wondered

with great admiration. (Rev 17:1-6)

— And the woman which thou sawest is that great city, which reigneth over the kings of the earth. (Rev 17:18)

— Now the Spirit speaketh expressly, that in the latter times some shall depart from the faith, giving heed to seducing spirits, and doctrines of devils.(1 Tim 4:1)

The third and the most popular church is the church of Satan that preaches and teaches the doctrine of devils using the Bible in deceiving their converts. This church is the mystery church revealed to the Apostle John in the Island of Patmos, as **BABYLON THE GREAT, THE MOTHER OF HARLOTS AND ABOMINATIONS OF THE EARTH.** It is the same church that Apostle Paul wrote about in Romans chapter one, in his letters to the saints of Jesus Christ who were in Rome during the time of his ministry in Rome. The test that reveals the True Church of Jesus Christ is not miracles or how numbered the people are, because Satan the god of this world and his demons do more miracles and wonders and also have the greatest number of congregation here on earth. --- *And he doeth great wonders, so that he maketh fire come down from heaven on the earth in the sight of men. And deceiveth them that dwell on the earth by the means of those miracles which he had power to do in the sight of the beast; saying to them that dwell on the earth, that they should make an image to the beast, which had the wound by a sword, and did live. (Rev 13:13-14)*

The Book of Revelations was written during the time that Rome ruled the whole world. In those days, The Romans had their own gods and their own ways of worshiping them, they were not going to allow another nation under their rulership introduce the worship of the Jewish God to the Romans, so they pretended to accept Christ so as to infiltrate Christianity and kill the Apostles and the early Christians, then they established their own churches premised on their owns doctrine which they invaded Jerusalem with. It is the doctrine that makes the difference and not the miracles, or the number of the congregation that is why we can still detect the deceivers by their doctrines. From the city of David (Jerusalem) came the DOCTRINE of Christ, where they preach and teach Jesus Christ the Lord God of the Jews and baptize their converts in His name for the remission of sins. Christianity started at Jerusalem as one family whose Father is Jesus Christ. It entered into Rome and turned to a religion by the Romans who never wanted trade their belief for another; so, they faked themselves as believers of the new Jewish faith in other to get the Christians killed and established their own faith which they introduced to the world as Christianity till date. — *And when they had brought them, they set them before the council: and the high priest asked them, Saying, did not we straitly command you that ye should not teach in this name? and, behold, ye have filled Jerusalem with your doctrine, and intend to bring this man's blood upon us. Then Peter and the other apostles answered and said, we ought to obey God rather than men. (Acts 5:27-29)*

— And they departed from the presence of the council, rejoicing that they were counted worthy to suffer shame for his name. And daily in the temple, and in every house, they ceased not to teach and preach Jesus Christ. (Acts 5:41-42)

The God of Abraham, Isaac and Jacob introduced Himself unto His people, the Jews as **ONE GOD** known unto them as Jehovah who every Jew must worship. Thus, the WINE of the woman's fornication found in the cup that she is holding and serving the whole world is the doctrine of TRINITY, idolatry, because God has never revealed Himself as God in three Persons to any of His Prophets. God is a Spirit and Holy by nature, He dwelt in Christ, the Son of God that came into the world as a **MAN** to save the world from their sins, then where is the position of the third Person in trinity? Jesus told Philip that He is in the Father and the Father is in him, and Apostle Paul also said God, the Father who is a Spirit and Holy in nature, was in Christ, who was the Son in the form of Flesh and blood, saving humanity from their sins as the Creator who came to save man His creature, then where is the place of third Person of the TRINITY?

Logically, one plus one is always equals to two and this is why the theologians and the Trinitarians can think they are right with their imaginations about the nature of the One True God of the Jews as being more than one person. Mathematically, one plus one cannot be equal to one, it is always two, as there is no two finger prints that is the same, and even twins no matter how they resemble themselves, there is a difference somewhere. It is only God who has the answer to the One plus One which is equals to One. This is what the Book of John chapter one the verse one, and the whole Book of the Revelation is all about, and this is what He meant when He told His disciples that I and my Father are One, because I am in the Father and the Father is in me. Jesus and His disciples proved the doctrine of trinity false before leaving the earth. That is why quoting the scriptures from Genesis 1:26-27 to confirm the argument of TRINITY is very wrong. Because, the image of God that He breathed into the nostril of MAN after He created him from the dust was His Spirit. That was what transformed him from a mold of dust to a living soul, and after man sinned, he died spiritually, and was separated from God who is essentially Spirit. The new birth is about washing the sinful SOULS of men in the blood-SOUL of Jesus Christ, and pouring His Living Spirit into the dead spirit of man giving him spiritual LIFE which is everlasting through BAPTISMS. This is what Jesus meant when He told Nicodemus to be born of water and Spirit and why no one can be saved without water and Spirit baptisms. Read the following scriptures to understand what Apostle Peter and Apostle Paul said about this matter:

For Christ also hath once suffered for sins, the just for the unjust, tht he might bring us to God, being put to death in the flesh, but quickened by the Spirit: By which also he went and preached unto the spirits in prison; Which sometime were disobedient, when once the longsuffering of God waited in the days of Noah, while the ark was a-preparing, wherein few, that is, eight souls were saved by water. The like figure whereunto even baptism doth also now save us (not the putting away of the filth of the flesh, but the answer of a good conscience toward God,) by the resurrection of Jesus Christ: (1 Peter 3:18-21)

— For to be carnally minded is death; but to be spiritually minded is life and peace. Because the carnal mind is enmity against God: for it is not

subject to the law of God, neither indeed can be. So then they that are in the flesh cannot please God. But ye are not in the flesh, but in the Spirit, if so be that the Spirit of God dwell in you. Now if any man have not the Spirit of Christ, he none of his. And if Christ be in you, the body is dead because of sin; but the Spirit is life because of righteousness. But if the Spirit of him that raised up Jesus from the dead dwell in you, he that raised up Christ from the dead shall also quicken your mortal bodies by his Spirit that dwelleth in you. (Rom 8:6-11)

CHAPTER TWO

FAITH AND UNDERSTANDING

— Now Faith is the substance of things hoped for, the evidence of things not seen. For by it the elders obtained a good report. Through faith we understand that the worlds were framed by the word of God, so that things which are seen were not made of things which do appear. (Heb 11:1-2)

— How then shall they call upon him in whom they have not believed? And how shall they believe in him of whom they have not heard? And how shall they hear without a preacher? And how shall they preach, except they be sent? As it is written, how beautiful are the feet of them that preach the gospel of peace, and bring glad tidings of good things! But they have not all obeyed the gospel. For Esaias saith, Lord, who hath believed our report? So, then faith cometh by hearing, and hearing by the word of God. (Rom 10:14-17)

The Bible says, "FAITH is the substance of things hoped for, the evidence of things not seen". The Bible goes further to say that without faith it is impossible to PLEASE the Lord. Faith and understanding are two separate words that are very important for every Christian in these last days if anyone wants to escape the damnation of hell. Faith is the foundation on which the Christian is connected or related to the invisible God, and the Bible says without it (faith) you can't please God. Faith is described as the SUBSTANCE of things hoped for, and the evidence of things not seen. If faith is the substance of the things we are hoping for as Christians but we don't see it until it happens, how then does FAITH work in creating the substance of the things we are hoping for?

As a matter of fact, faith cannot be held or touched until it produces the created substance which can now be seen and be touched. Faith is the creative power that gets into the spirit of man through the soul to create what God wants to create in the midst of people and to show forth His existence or glory. Faith comes by hearing the word of God in these three areas: the past i.e. what God did in the past; the present, what God is doing now; the future, what God is going to do. Believe it or not it is based on God's WORD that man knows his beginning and his destination after death.

The Book of Hebrews explained the efficacy of faith; it is through the hearing and believing of God's word that His creative power starts to work in those who believe that impossible things are possible through the creative power of God's word. So holding unto that strong belief, they get the reality of their faith through the given substance from where they start praising God for what He has done for them.

Although reading the Old Testament produces faith for greater works in the Lord but there are two strong occasions that Jesus acted on in the New Testament that will help us as Christians if we can build our trust in God upon these two scriptures.

— Then Jesus went with them. And when he was now not far from the house, the centurion sent friends to him, saying unto him, Lord, trouble not thyself: for I am not worthy that thou shouldest enter under my roof: Wherefore neither thought I myself worthy to come unto thee: but say in a word, and my servant shall be healed. For I also am a man set under authority, having under me soldiers, and I say unto one, Go, and he goeth; and to another, Come, and he cometh; and to my servant, Do this, and he doeth it. When Jesus heard these things, he marveled at him, and turned him about, and said unto the people that followed him, I say unto you, I have not found so great faith, no, not in Israel. And they that were sent, returning to the house, found the servant whole that had been sick. (Luke 7:6-10)

— Now when he had left speaking, he said unto Simon, Launch out into the deep, and let down your nets for a draught. And Simon answering said unto him, Master, we have toiled all the right, and have taken nothing: nevertheless at thy world I will let down the net. And when they had this done, they enclosed a great multitude of fishes: and their net brake. (Luke 5:4-6)

The above scriptures give us the understanding in two ways: how the impossible can become possible through belief in and obedience to the WORD of God. Another way is to speak out boldly what you want to see through the WORD. The Lord commanded Peter to cast his net for a catch, and because he obeyed Peter and his companion caught a multitude of fish. Faith demands action if you want to see the results of your faith. You don't need to see the result before you act on faith, otherwise, faith is needless, because it is the faith that produces the result you need. That is why many Christians who are waiting to see before they believe have become unbelieving believers. If we want to walk with the Lord victoriously, we must combine faith and understanding, because faith empowers the believer while understanding unveils mysteries on their way to glory.

The Bible says faith cometh by hearing, and hearing by the WORD of God. It is written that we overcame the world by our faith, so as Christians if we want to live a victorious life in the Lord and in this evil world, we must feed our faith with the word of God so that we can overcome every unpleasant situation that the devil and his demons may bring our way. It is the result of our faith that establishes the substance for our understanding; that is why without it no one can please the Lord. Faith enters into the spiritual realm and supernaturally pulls out what you are expecting with a force of authority that can`t be stopped by any spiritual force if it is declared by the word of God.

The Bible says whosoever shall come unto the Lord must first believe that He exists and is a rewarder of those who diligently seek Him. The Lord Jesus Christ told the Apostles, *"that without me ye can do nothing."* Peter discovered that faith in the Lord and in His word is the only way a disciple of Jesus Christ can accomplish his goal so he told the lame man at the gate of the temple called Beautiful that, silver and gold I have none, but what I have I give to you, in the name of Jesus Christ of Nazareth rise up and walk.

Today the devil has succeeded in putting many Christians in the prison of fear and doubt; that is why many are not seeing the glory of God in their lives. People go from seminars to seminars, crusade to crusade and get fully loaded with the written WORD of God, but cannot act upon the WORD or speak out because of doubt and fear. If the Holy Spirit tells a Christian to just speak by faith for God to show forth His glory, the devil would also speak to the same person that, if you speak and nothing happens, is that not a disgrace? Many are still under the control of the devil in this area that is why many ministers of God's word are getting fed up with the ministry.

God said *"I am the Lord I changeth not".* James had made the matter clear for us by saying Elijah was a man like us who prayed that there should be no rain for three years and it was so, he prayed again and there was rain.

God took Ezekiel into a place of dry bones and asked him, "can these dry bones live, son of man?", Ezekiel replied *"Thou knowest".* From there the Lord commanded him to speak from one stage to another until he saw the dry bones as a great army which has come to pass in Israel today making it a nation after a long period of desolation. In short, the Lord has deposited great things in His children today than ever before but fear and doubt block us in so many ways simple because we want to see before we believe.

Many preachers and teachers talk more about doubting Thomas, but the fact is that the Church today doubts God more than Thomas, because we want to see before we can act on our faith. That is why we don't act in faith at all.

In Christianity our understanding of the things of God gets developed daily if we keep walking in faith, so the Bible says the just shall live by his faith. God told His people to go and possess the land on which He knew there were giants who would try to stop them, yet He told them to go and possess it despite the giants. Their failure as the people of God was that they did not size up the giants against the WORD of God but sized themselves against the giants and that's why they saw themselves as grass hoppers before their enemies. When Joshua and Caleb sized the giants with the WORD of God they saw the giants as grass hoppers so they motivated the people to go and possess the land. God has given us many things to posses so if we don't see things with the eyes of FAITH we would miss a lot of blessings. Lack of faith in God's word is what is leading many Christians into bondage under the leadership of the false prophets who are increasing daily throughout the world.

It is time to awake and feed our soul and spirit with the word of God so that we can walk as overcomers in the Lord. If you want to understand before you act on faith you will miss it, just act in faith according to the word of God, and the result would give you the understanding you are looking for, because God is angry with those who doubt Him, so it is time to hold onto the shield of FAITH so that you can quench the fiery darts of the enemy. — ***And the LORD said unto Moses, how long will this people provoke me? And how long will it be ere they believe me, for all the signs which I have shown among them? I will smite them with the pestilence, and disinherit them, and will make of thee a greater nation and mightier than they. (Num 14:11-12)***

The story in the Book of Numbers chapter 14 will help us to understand that God hates people who doubt Him but deceive themselves that they are walking with Him by faith. If Moses did not intercede for the people, God would have destroyed them and out of Moses, raised up another generation and from this, the enemies would have a message to preach against God, by saying because He could not take the people to the promise land He killed all of them in the wilderness.

The church today doesn't know that lack of faith is destroying her, so she goes about things that cannot help her; this is the main reason why the children of God are chasing these false prophets here and there seeking help that turns to more problems, because they stop seeking God and instead begin to follow human beings who continue to deceive them. If you lack faith ask the Lord in prayer to increase your faith as the Apostles of old did.

CHAPTER THREE

POWER AND REVELATION

It is not how powerful you are as a man of God that matters, but God's given revelation to you is what matters. The Lord Jesus Christ after calling the twelve gave them power to cast out unclean spirits, but after the resurrection, he opened their understanding to understand the scriptures. The scriptures stated that God by wisdom founded the earth but by understanding established it, so for Jesus to establish a permanent relationship with His chosen people He opened their understanding scriptures. — **Then He called his twelve disciples together, and gave them power and authority over all devils, and to cure diseases. (Luke 9:1)**

Power and revelation are two different things with the Lord. A Christian may have power and back it up with faith, cast out all devils, remove mountains and even do greater works as Jesus stated in the scriptures, but will lack revelation and knowledge. That is why the Bible says, *"for lack of knowledge my people perish"* Power of faith in Jesus Christ will give you boldness, but revelation will give you the knowledge of the TRUTH, which is the liberating agent of freedom from deceivers, and not power.

From the above scripture Jesus Christ gave His disciples power and authority to cast out devils while He was with them. We should remember that the seventy disciples that Jesus gave authority and power to cast out demons came to Him with joy that devils were subject unto them. But Jesus told them not to be happy because demons were subject unto them, but they should rejoice because their names are written in the Book of Life. Jesus Christ has given to the Church the needed truth of how the end shall be, by saying that day many shall say unto Him, *"in your name we cast out demons and healed the sick, and done many wonderful works"* and the

Lord says He will tell them I don't know you, you workers of iniquity.

Remember, it takes power and faith to cast out demons and heal the sick or do wonderful works in the Lord, but all these the Lord will say unto some "I know you not". Since the day of Pentecost the Lord gave power unto the church, so the church of Jesus Christ is still being sustained by the power of God even till Rapture, just like Simeon who was in Jerusalem, before the birth of Jesus Christ to whom the Holy Spirit revealed to, that he would not die until he saw the Lord's Christ. He was sustained by the power of God but to see the Lord's Christ it was through revelation — **And, behold, there was a man in Jerusalem, whose name was Simeon and the same man was just and devout, waiting for the consolation of Israel, and the Holy Ghost was upon him. And it was revealed unto him by the Holy Ghost, that he should not see death before he had seen the Lord's Christ. (Luke 2:25-26)**

Just like Simeon, in Jerusalem who got the revelation of the Lord's Christ before his death, many are in Church today who need the revelation of the Lord's Christ before they die or before the Rapture. Many Christians are fasting and praying for power to do miracles in the name of the Lord Jesus Christ but are not praying for the revelation of Who the power giver is. They are not praying for the revelation of Jesus Christ like in the Book of Revelation where Jesus revealed Himself unto John, as the first and the last and I am. This is why many are still believing the Trinity, God in three persons **"blessed trinity"**. When Apostle Paul got the revelation of Jesus Christ on the way to Damascus, he did not see Trinity, God the father, God the Son, God the Holy Ghost, but he saw that the Father became the Son (put on flesh and blood) to save His own children as Jesus Christ and this is what he called the MYSTERY OF GODLINESS, that God was manifested in the flesh. If there is One God who manifested in the flesh then where is Trinity or how came the DOCTRINE of this Trinity if not from the devil?

Satan, knowing that in the last days before the Rapture, people will start knowing the TRUTH has established another doctrine to keep the children of God in bondage which he called the **"unholy trinity".** When the writer of the Book of Revelation got the revelation of the last Book of the Bible, revealing what Daniel sealed in the Bible, he did not see trinity but saw Jesus who came and died for us just like what Apostle Paul also saw. Even today, for whomsoever the God of heaven will reveal Himself unto, who they see is Jesus. You may be walking with the Lord by faith and power but that is not enough, you need revelation of Who He is, because a son needs to know his father. You may say, some children don't know their fathers or parents, but remember it is written that bastards shall not enter into the congregation of the Lord. **Please we are not talking about physical fathers here,** We are born again into the kingdom of our Lord and Father Jesus Christ in His NAME, as the members of the heavenly family. Read the following scriptures and pray that God should open your heart to understand the scriptures which you have been witnessing to people to know if you indeed are witnessing rightly. During the days of our Lord Jesus a lot was said about His identity which never was, so it is in these last days many are preaching Jesus but has not got the revelation of who He is.

— And he said unto them, these are the words which I spake unto you, while I was yet with you, that all things must be fulfilled, which were written in the law of Moses, and in the prophets, and in the Psalms, concerning me. Then opened he their understanding, that they might understand the scriptures, and said unto them, thus it is written, and thus it behooved Christ to suffer, and to rise from the dead the third day, and that repentance and remission of sins should be preached in his name among all nations, beginning at Jerusalem, and ye are witnesses of these things. (Luke 24:44-48)

From the Book of Luke 9:1 we read that, the people (disciples) were given power and authority over devils and to cure diseases but the final thing the Lord did unto His disciples before He left them was to open their understanding of scriptures by knowing Who Jesus is; that is why they did not go about baptizing anybody in the name of the Father, and of the Son, and of the Holy Ghost, but baptized their converts in Jesus' Name **FOR THE REMISSION OF SINS**. Many today are exercising the power of Christianity in Jesus' name but have not got the revelation of whom He is; thus many have refused to be re-baptized in His NAME for the remission of their sins, and since they have refused their sins are still not remitted because the only Baptism in the New Testament for a sinner is to be baptized in Jesus' name for the remission of sins. Since the Bible says all have sinned and have come short of the glory of God, baptism in Jesus' name will wash away that sin, so seek to be baptized in Jesus' name for the remission of your sins, before the Lord will tell you to go away from him, *"you that worketh iniquity"* because on the judgment day the sins of those Christians who have refused to be baptized in Jesus' Name will be shown. You may ask what about those who baptized in the Name of the Father, of the Son and of the Holy Spirit?

That should have been a very good question, if Peter did not say, "save yourself from this untoward generation". Salvation is for individuals so if you hear the word of God harden not your heart. That is why you are to leave that question and do the right thing as it is revealed unto you from the scriptures, because Peter got to know who Jesus is through revelation, likewise Paul. That is why the Bible says the Son of God has come and given us understanding. The revelation of our salvation is in the SON (Jesus Christ) who shared His BLOOD (Life) for our redemption. You may exercise your FAITH in His Name, and see the result of the power of you faith, but still lack salvation in His Name. So the Bible says —*And this is the record, that God hath given to us eternal life, and this life is in his Son. He that hath the Son hath life; and he that hath not the Son of God hath not life. These things have I written unto you that believe on the name of the Son of God; that ye may know that ye have eternal life, and that ye may believe on the name of the Son of God. (1 John 5:11-13)*

CHAPTER FOUR

THE MYSTERIES OF THE CHRISTIAN FAITH

Eph 3:1-9 --- For this cause I Paul, the prisoner of Jesus Christ for you Gentiles, If ye have heard of the dispensation of the grace of God which is given me to you-ward: How that by revelation he made known unto me the mystery; (as I wrote afore in few words, Whereby, when ye read, ye may understand my knowledge in the mystery of Christ) Which in other ages was not made known unto the sons of men, as it is now revealed unto his holy apostles and prophets by the Spirit; That the Gentiles should be fellow heirs, and of the same body, and partakers of his promise in Christ by the gospel: Whereof I was made a minister, according to the gift of the grace of God given unto me by the effectual working of his power. Unto me, who am less than the least of all saints, is this grace given, that I should preach among the Gentiles the unsearchable riches of Christ; And to make all men see what is the fellowship of the mystery, which from the beginning of the world hath been hid in God, who created all things by Jesus Christ.

--- Likewise, must the deacons be grave, not double tongued, not given to much wine, not greedy of filthy lucre. Holding the mystery of the faith in a pure conscience. (1 Tim 3:8-9)

--- But if I tarry long, that thou mayest know how thou oughtest to behave thyself in the house of God, which is the church of the living God, the pillar and ground of the truth. And without controversy great is the mystery of godliness, God was manifest in the flesh, justified in the Spirit, seen of angels, preached unto the Gentiles, believed on in the world, received up into glory. (1 Tim 3:15-16)

As sons and daughters of God, to resist diversion from the Truth, we must pay attention to Paul's letters to the churches, and especially his letter to his son

Timothy whom he used as the road model to lead the sons and daughters of the Lord unto God himself. From the above scriptures Timothy's father and teacher in the Lord wrote unto him, how he must behave himself in the house of God which is the church of the living God, the pillar and the ground of the truth. He continued by telling him that without disputation God was manifested in the flesh, justified in the Spirit, seen of angels and preached unto the Gentiles and received up into glory.

The Apostle was chosen by God's divine voice of hearing, seeing and understanding. As a chosen one among persecutors the Lord Jesus Christ revealed himself unto him by sight (revelation) and voice (speech) while others around him, heard the voice but saw no one. As a son, Timothy was given the apostolic voice, the Word that became flesh (Jesus) to preach for people's salvation. He was also given the revelation of whom the WORD that he was to preach is, and to make him different from others who may preach the Word (Jesus) without revelation, he told him not to dispute with anybody about the given, revelation of the mystery of godliness, which is the One true God, coming into this world as a man to save a fallen man by dying on his stead. This is done for the fulfillment of the scripture in Deuteronomy.

--- *The secret things belong unto the Lord our God, but those things which are revealed belong unto us and to our children for ever, that we may do all the words of this law. (Deut. 29:29)* The secret thing that was revealed unto Apostle Paul to share or give unto his children, sons and daughters in the Lord is the MYSTERY OF GODLINESS which is the Creator of man becoming a man his creature. This mystery was hidden from the disciples of Jesus Christ who walked and even ate with Him until His death, burial and resurrection. Having finished his purpose of coming into the world he opened their understanding of scriptures, because they were being commissioned to go and preach salvation to the lost world, so they must know exactly what to preach to save their followers.

Since this remained a mystery unto apostle Paul and some of his fellow Jews, they thought the disciples were blaspheming so they teamed up to stop that message which is for mankind's salvation, thinking they were doing the work of God (the God of their fathers.) But among the persecutors, Paul found mercy in the sight of God, so God revealed Himself to him as Jesus Christ whom he was persecuting and told him that he was chosen to carry His Name unto the Gentiles. The mystery behind the Christian faith is the manifestation of God in the flesh. Paul got the revelation of the mystery of the truth about whom Jesus is, but his first message about Jesus at Damascus in the synagogues was that, Christ is the Son of God.

--- And straightway he preached Christ in the synagogues, that he is the Son of God. But all that heard him were amazed, and said, is not this he that destroyed them which called on this name in Jerusalem and came hither for that intent, that he might bring them bound unto the chief priests? (Acts 9:20-21) The Lord revealed himself to Paul on the way to Damascus as Jesus, but at his first message in the synagogue, he preached Christ is the Son of God. Understanding his first message about the Christ would help remove the confusion of Who Jesus is from your mind. The Christ we know is the anointed body that is referred to as the Son of God in which the Father, who is a SPIRIT with the name Jesus, dwelled on this earth to save his people. Thus, that makes him the Father and at the same time the Son. If we understand him as the Father and at the same time the Son it will help us to understand how he is described in the book of Revelation as the Lion of the tribe of Judah and at the same time the Lamb of God, because he became a Son to save his sons and daughters. He is a Lamb giving birth to lambs and a Lion taking care of his lambs (sheep), and dwells in them as the Holy Ghost, that is why the Bible says greater is He that dwells in you than he that is in the world.

CHAPTER FIVE

THE MANIFESTATION OF THE ETERNAL LIFE

— *That which was from the beginning which we have heard, which we have seen, with our eyes, which we have looked upon, and our hands have handled, of the Word of life; (For the life was manifested, and we have seen it, and bear witness, and show unto you that eternal life, which was with the Father, and was manifested unto us;) (1 John 1:1-2)*

— *For whatsoever is born of God overcometh the world and this is the victory that overcometh the world, even our faith. Who is he that overcometh the world, but he that believeth that Jesus is the Son of God? This is he that came by water and blood, even Jesus Christ; not by water only, but by water and blood. And it is the Spirit that beareth witness, because the Spirit is truth. For there are three that bear record in heaven, the Father, the Word, and the Holy Ghost, and these tree are one. And there are three that bear witness in earth, the spirit, and the water, and the blood; and these three agree in one. (1 John 5:4-8)*

— *And this is the record, that God hath given to us eternal life, and this life is in his Son. He that hath the Son hath life; and he that hath not the Son of God hath not life. These things have I written unto you that believe on the name of the Son of God; that ye may know that ye have eternal life, and that ye may believe on the name of the Son of God. (1John 5:11-13)*

It is written that **"the entrance of thy WORD, bringeth light"** and **"thy WORD is a lamp unto my feet".** As a matter of fact, many great men of God, who entered into the Word of God and founded their own churches, have left behind confusion that can never be solved. They forgot that, Satan the old serpent knows the WORD of God more than any man of God that had ever passed through this earth, that is why he tempted Jesus (the WORD that became flesh) with "it is written", of which Jesus also replied him with "it is written". These two *"it is written"* are the main weapons of war in the church of God today, that is why if you are waiting for these religious wars to cease before you search for the TRUE CHURCH of Jesus Christ you will not but go to hell. This war shall never cease because the devil is also looking for converts for hell.

Jesus told His disciples in the Bible, from **Matt 13:11**, that "for unto you it is given to know the mysteries of the kingdom of heaven, but unto them it is not given" because it is not given unto them to understand the mysteries of the kingdom, it shall remain a parable unto them. In short Jesus is behind "it is written" and Satan is also behind "it is written". That is why these religious wars shall never cease until God does all things new. The victory of the Christians is the revelation of the mystery on the part of Jesus and His children; this will ever remain a mystery unto the devil and his children in this battle field, until the Rapture. Based on this understanding let's seek God's mercy through the scriptures for the revelation of the hidden mystery of our salvation through the above scriptures. Since the Bible interprets itself let's pick some keys of understanding from **Hebrew 1:1-2** so that when we enter into the above given scriptures the devil would not divert us by giving unto us his understanding that leads from the narrow way to the broad way into destruction.

— God who at Sundry times and in divers manners spake in time past unto the fathers by the prophets, hath in these last days spoken unto us by his Son, whom he hath appointed heir of all things, by whom also he made the worlds. (Hebrews 1:1-2)

In the books of Hebrews and John, the identity of Jesus Christ of Nazareth is revealed as the same Jehovah in the Old Testament who delivered the Jews from the hands of Pharaoh and the Egyptians.

The scriptures says: God (Jehovah) who of old and in diverse manners (different ways) spoke in time past unto the fathers (the Jewish fathers) by the Prophets, has in these last days spoken unto us by His Son (who is Jesus Christ.) The key to understand that Jesus Christ, is the Almighty God who came in the flesh has already been given unto the chosen (the elect,) so you are either part of them or not no matter how religious you may think you are or how many miracles you do a day. God has spoken through the scriptures, that He created all things, all alone and there is no God beside Him, He knows no other God beside Him, He is all alone the Almighty God.

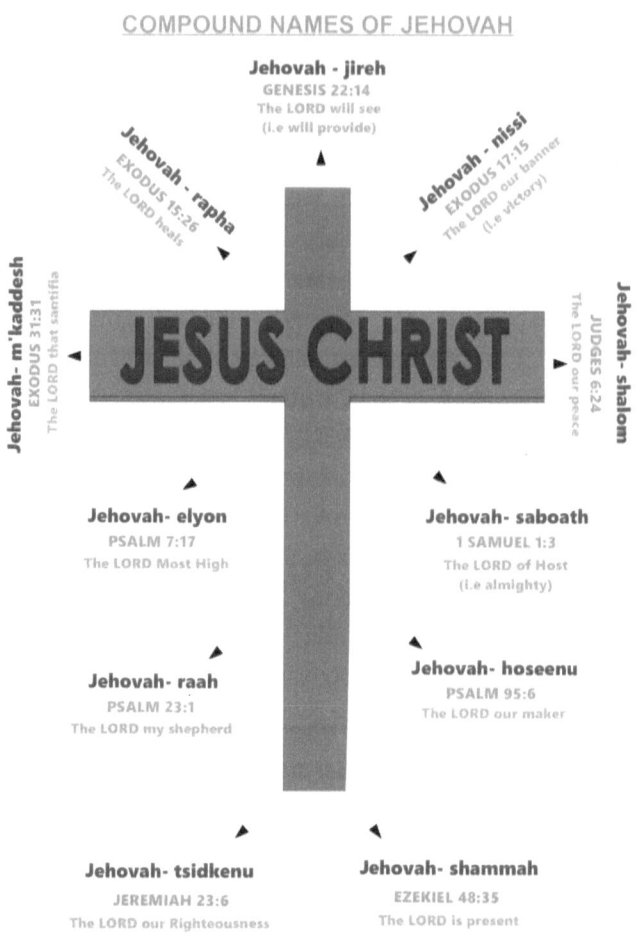

To be saved from the hands of these religious men in our days which the Bible calls the last days, it takes the grace and the mercy of God that is why our cry unto the Lord must be "Oh! Lord save me by your truth in Jesus name. Amen". It is one thing to choose to serve the Lord and it is another thing for God to call and choose you, for his work; think about it! Those whom the Lord calls or chooses he reveals the mysteries of the kingdom unto them so they are without confusion to understand the things of the kingdom and the King who rules in the kingdom. The manifestation of God in the flesh as a Son is well explained in the book of Hebrews and in the book of John, and as the Lord said he will speak in parables when he comes in the flesh, the book of Hebrews chapter 7 has something to say about Melchisedec, the King of righteousness and peace unto the children of God. Let's see from the scriptures for confirmation. ***Hebrews 7:1-4 — For this Melchisedec, king of Salem, priest of the most high God, who met Abraham returning from the slaughter of the kings, and bless him; To whom also Abraham gave a tenth part of all; first being by interpretation King of righteousness, and after that also King of Salem, which is , King of peace; Without father, without mother, without descent, having neither beginning of days, nor end of life; but made like unto the Son of God; abideth a priest continually. Now consider how great this man was, unto whom even the patriarch Abraham gave the tenth of the spoil.***

The Apostle John wrote unto the Church of Jesus Christ, that "there are three that bear record in heaven, the Father, the Word, and the Holy Ghost, and these three are one". He continued to say "there are three that bear witness on the earth: the spirit, the water, and the blood, and these three agree in one. For many years now after the death of the original Apostles of Jesus Christ, the devil has succeeded in creating his own doctrine within the Apostolic doctrine (the doctrine of Christ) just as how he did it in the Garden of Eden to deceive Eve and Adam, by creating the belief of TRINITY, God in three persons which is being interpreted and taught in the church of Jesus Christ as God the Father, God the Son, and God the Holy Ghost.

If you can remember that Satan tempted Jesus Christ with the Word of God from *Ps 91:11-12* then this study will do you good if you want. The devil has so many tricks in deceiving the people of God to believe in his lies. I have heard a man of God who confirmed the doctrine of Trinity with Genesis 18 by saying God the Father, God the Son and God the Holy Ghost were the people who visited Abraham when going to destroy Sodom and Gomorrah. The devil quoted from the Old Testament to tempt Jesus Christ. If there are any scriptures the Old serpent has given to some Christians to destroy themselves with, they are **Matt. 28:19 and 1 John 5:7.**

The writings of the Apostles did not contradict themselves because it was given unto them to understand the mysteries of the kingdom of Heaven, and so if we are confused by their words it is left for us because they did not leave behind any confusion at all. Apostle Matthew recorded the word that came out from the mouth of Jesus Christ accurately without adding to them or removing from them, so if we remove or add to them we will answer for ourselves. Let's trace the scriptures as we compare them, and God by his mercy will give us understanding. — *Go ye therefore, and teach all nations, baptizing them in the name of the Father, and of the Son, and of the Holy Ghost. Teaching them to observe all things whatsoever I have commanded you and lo, I am with you always, even unto the end of the world Amen. (Matt 28:19-20)*

— And this is the record, that God hath given to us eternal life, and this life is in his Son. He that hath the Son hath life, and he that hath not the Son of God hath not life. These things have I written unto you that believe on the name of the Son of God, that ye may know that ye have eternal life, and that ye may believe on the name of the Son of God. (1 John 5:11-13)

The commandment that Jesus gave unto his disciples which Matthew recorded is this "Go ye therefore, and teach all nations, baptizing them in the NAME of the Father, and of the Son and of the Holy Ghost. Before Matthew recorded the above scripture, Jesus Christ had given unto them the understanding of the mysteries of the kingdom of heaven, and including the *NAME* of the Father, when he was with them, calling God his Father. The commandment of *Matthew 28:19-20* is not for us Christians today, but was a commandment given unto the eleven Apostles (after the fall of Judas Iscariot) who will teach the world what Jesus Christ taught them. Many men of God have ignorantly quoted this scripture to their own destruction and the destruction of their followers. Believe it or not, the truth about God's word cannot be changed.

It was the commandment of Jesus Christ which is recorded by some of the Apostles (the four gospels) that gave birth to the book of Acts where the foundation of the Church can be traced. As a matter of fact our relationship with Jesus Christ without the Apostles teachings (doctrine) is no other thing than acting upon a deceitful faith that leads to a ditch. In the Church today, we have some self-appointed Apostles who are not connected to Jesus Christ through His apostles. These sorts of apostles have been from the very beginning and Apostle Paul wrote about them, in his letters to the churches.

I have heard men of God ask if we should believe what Peter said in the Book of *Acts 2:38* or what is written in *Matt 28:19?* This in fact is a childish question if you can get the understanding. Don't be deceived; the relationship of the Apostles who walked and ate with Jesus Christ is completely different from the so called 'Apostles' of today. So, if a man of God can ask a question that, "should we believe the word of Apostle Peter or Jesus Christ", this is to tell us that if these people were to be with Jesus Christ in His days they would ask, "should we believe God or Jesus Christ?" Please pray for the understanding of the following statement; Jesus said, *"no one goes to the Father but, by me"*. Apostle Paul wrote that God was in Christ reconciling the whole world unto Himself. I may also say "Jesus Christ is in His disciples of today reconciling the whole world unto Himself." That is why He said I will come and dwell in you until the end of the world. Please, let's read the following scriptures so that you can understand that there are some statements in the Bible which are for specific people, for special duties.

— Then the eleven disciples went away into Galilee, into a mountain where Jesus had appointed them. And when they saw him, they worshipped him, but some doubted. And Jesus came and spake unto them, saying, all power is given unto me in heaven and in earth. Go ye therefore, and teach all nations baptizing them in the name of the Father, and of the Son and of the Holy Ghost. Teaching them to observe all things whatsoever I have commanded you, and lo, I am with you always even unto the end of the world. Amen. (Matt 28:16-20)

If we read God's word and study it well, with a humble heart, God will always give us the understanding which He wants us to have. If you read *Matt. 28:16-20,* you will see from these scriptures that, they were for the eleven disciples whom Jesus gave the command that in obeying, gave birth to the Church in the book of Acts (acting on the commandment.)

Even among the disciples of Jesus Christ, it was not all of them who witnessed the transfiguration; it was only Peter, James and John whom the Lord chose to reveal that to, or gave that special grace to, and after He told them to keep the vision until His resurrection from the dead. In *Matt. 28:19*, the above commandment was given before the call of Matthias, who was chosen by the Lord Jesus Christ Himself to replace Judas Iscariot who betrayed his master, Jesus Christ. The understanding of the mysteries of the kingdom of God was given unto the disciples of Jesus Christ to go and preach the gospel to all nations of which we are apart, for the fulfillment of God's covenant with our father Abraham that *"I will make you the father of many nations"*

The disciples were commanded to teach their converts what He has given unto them through His teachings, so if today we have converts who are teaching the Apostles of Jesus Christ, it is no other spirit than the spirit of the antichrist who is preparing the way for the antichrist who is going to be revealed in these days, because the spirit of the antichrist goes contrary to the Spirit of Christ, who is Jesus Christ Himself, who dwells in His people as the Holy Spirit.

CHAPTER SIX

THE TRUE GOD AND ETERNAL LIFE

— We know that whosoever is born of God sinneth not, but he that is begotten of God keepeth himself, and that wicked one toucheth him not. And we know that we are of God, and the whole world lieth in wickedness. And we know that the Son of God is come, and hath given us an understanding, that we may know him that is true, and we are in him that is true, even in his Son Jesus Christ. This is the true God, and eternal life. Little children, keep yourselves from idols. Amen. (1 John 5:18-21)

— As thou hast given him power over all flesh, that he should give eternal life to as many as thou hast given him. And this is life eternal, that they might know thee the only true God, and Jesus Christ, whom thou hast sent. (John 17:2-3)

— Jer. 10:10 But the Lord is the true God, he is the living God, and an everlasting king: at his wrath the earth shall tremble, and the nations shall not be able to abide his indignation. (Jer. 10:10)

Jesus Christ told the Jews that Salvation of man is premised on the knowledge of the One true God whose name is Jesus. ***"If you don't believe that I am He, you shall die in your sins"***. He continued and told them that *"I am the way, the truth, and the life, no one goes to the Father but by me"*

From Genesis to Revelation, the Bible teaches that there is only One true God who created heaven and earth all alone. It also teaches that there is only one Satan (a fallen angel) and his demons (fallen angels) who supported Satan when he rebelled against God. We have never come across Satan in three persons ***"cursed unholy Trinity"***; it is the same Satan who corrupted the word of God given unto Adam and Eve in the Garden of Eden and caused their fall. In the wilderness, he corrupted the WORD of God and quoted it to Jesus Christ to cause His downfall.

Since Satan fell from his position in heaven, he and his followers keep trying to corrupt the word of God so as to conscript as disciples into his followership. Satan has succeeded in leading many people to believe that there is trinity, by corruption and misconstruing *Matt 28:19* and other scriptures, he deceives many men of God saying that even Jesus Christ taught the doctrine of trinity, God the Father, God the Son, and God the Holy Ghost. Please don't let the devil to deceive you. The Bible teaches the existence of only One true God who is the Creator of everything. *--- **Thou believest that there is one God, thou doest well, the devils also believe, and tremble. (James 2:19)***

Jesus said in John 17:3 that *"this is life eternal, that they might know thee the only true God, and Jesus Christ, whom thou hast sent"*. The belief in Trinity and its explanation of God the Father, God the Son, and God the Holy Ghost is a religious faith and not the Christian faith. The Christian faith teaches that Jesus Christ is the Father who became the Son, to save His sons and daughters who are flesh and blood, by washing away their sins with His own blood, and to dwell in them as the Holy Ghost that they may be His children while in this sinful and cursed world.

*— **Forasmuch then as the children are partakers of flesh and blood, he also himself likewise took part of the same, that through death he might destroy him that had the power of death, that is, the devil. And deliver then who through fear of death were all their lifetime subject to bondage. For verily he took not on him the nature of angels, but he took on him the seed of Abraham. (Heb 2:14-16)***

The foundation of the Christian faith is accepting and confessing Jesus Christ as your personal Lord and Savior for your salvation and nothing else that is why the Bible says: Jesus Christ is the TRUE GOD AND ETERNAL LIFE. Now, I want to throw a challenge to you, search the scriptures and see if you can find anywhere in the Bible where any of the early Apostles of Jesus Christ baptized any of their converts in the Name of the Father, and of the Son and of the Holy Ghost. If yes, then continue to believe in Trinity but if no, why do you still believe in Trinity if the Bible teaches the existence of One True God?

JESUS WAS THE CHRIST- THE SON OF GOD

*— **And when Silas and Timotheus were come from Macedonia, Paul was pressed in the spirit, and testified to the Jews that Jesus was Christ.***

— And a certain Jew named Apollos, born at Alexandria, an eloquent man, and mighty in the scriptures, came to Ephesus. This man was instructed in the way of the Lord; and being fervent in the spirit, he spake and taught diligently the things of the Lord, knowing only the baptism of John. And he began to speak boldly in the synagogue: whom when Aquila and Priscilla had heard, they took him unto them, and expounded unto him the way of God more perfectly. And when he was disposed to pass into Achaia, the brethren wrote, exhorting the disciples to receive him: who, when he was come, helped them much which had believed through grace. For he mightily convinced the Jews, and that publicly, showing by the scriptures that Jesus was Christ. (Acts 18:5, 24-28)

The statement 'Jesus was the Christ' introduces two separate realities and positions which needs to be properly explained to those who are ministers the Gospel, because this is where the whole mystery of godliness is. The position of the CHRIST in the life of Jesus and His ministry is now a past tense right after His resurrection from the dead. According to the testimonies that His disciples gave concerning the **CHRIST**, *the Christ* was the anointed Body in which Jesus who is the eternal Spirit and the Father of all creations dwelt in this sinful and cursed world. We could see that His disciples gave a testimony of the work He did through the Christ while on earth and after He finished His work as the Christ, He entered His glory as the King of kings and the Lord of lords and is no more the Christ or the Son of God. This is what Apostle Paul by revelation wrote for our understanding that *"God was in Christ reconciling the world unto Himself";* it is the same message that joined Apollos to the disciples of Jesus Christ and is still joining people to Christ before His return. The work of the Son has got nothing to do in Heaven but here on earth because there are no sinners in Heaven who need salvation. Therefore, those who think they are going to Heaven to see God the Father, God the Son and God the Holy Ghost would see only Jesus, the King of kings and the Lord of lords.

— Now when the centurion, and they that were with him, watching Jesus, saw the earthquake, and those things that were done, they feared greatly, saying, Truly this was the Son of God. (Matt 27:54)

— And when I saw him, I fell at his feet as dead. And he laid his right hand upon me, saying unto me, Fear not; I am the first and the last: I am he that liveth, and was

dead; and, behold, I am alive for evermore, Amen; and have the keys of hell and of death. (Rev 1:17-18)

Our loving Father, Jesus Christ is not the author of confusion. On the cross where He gave up the ghost for our salvation, people who stood aside and watched gave a testimony about Him that truly He was the Son of God. Some years after His resurrection, He revealed Himself unto Apostle John on the island of Patmos and confirmed to him that He was the One who died and resurrected again. In short, the position of Jesus Christ as the Son of God for our salvation could be found only here on earth, in heaven He is sitting upon the Throne and receiving praises and worship from His children the saints and the redeemed. Let's see from the scriptures what Apostle Paul wrote down to the saints about Him.

— And straightway he preached Christ in the synagogues, that he is the Son of God. But all that heard him were amazed, and said; Is not this he that destroyed them which called on this name in Jerusalem, and came hither for that intent, that he might bring them bound unto the chief priests? But Saul increased the more in strength, and confounded the Jews which dwelt at Damascus, proving that this is very Christ. And after that many days were fulfilled; the Jews took counsel to kill him. (Acts 9:20-23)

These things write I unto thee, hoping to come unto thee shortly: But if I tarry long, that thou mayest know how thou oughtest to behave thyself in the house of God, which is the church of the living God, the pillar and ground of the truth. And without controversy great is the mystery of godliness: God was manifest in the flesh, justified in the Spirit, seen of angels, preached unto the Gentiles, believed on in the world, received up into glory. (1 Timothy 3:14-16)

Ye are my witnesses, saith the LORD, and my servant whom I have chosen: that ye may know and believe me and understand that I am he: before me there was no God formed, neither shall there be after me. I, even I, am the LORD; and beside me there is no Savior. I have declared, and have saved, and I have shown, when there was no strange god among you: therefore, ye are my witnesses, saith the LORD, that I am God. Yea, before the day was I am he; and there is none that can deliver out of my hand: I will work, and who shall let it? Thus, saith the LORD, your redeemer, the Holy One of Israel; For your sake I have sent to Babylon, and have brought down all their nobles, and the Chaldeans, whose cry is in the ships. I am the LORD, your Holy One, the creator of Israel, your King. (Is 43:10-15)

Yet I am the LORD thy God from the land of Egypt, and thou shalt know no god but me: for there is no Savior beside me. I did know thee in the wilderness, in the land of great drought. (Hosea 13:4-5)

Finally, we can now see plainly from the scriptures that, there is One God who is Spirit and Holy in nature, who alone shed His Blood for humanity, saving them from their sins and poured His Spirit upon them. Understanding the above scriptures brings victory for every true man and child of God, in this religious and confused world where Satan is also seeking souls for Hell. It is plainly revealed in the pages of the scriptures that, Jesus Christ of Nazareth is the Creator and the Savior of the world, and that qualifies Him as the One True God-the Creator and the Eternal Life the-Savior.

CHAPTER SEVEN

THE CHURCH OF JESUS CHRIST IS MARRIED TO JESUS CHRIST.

— For I am jealous over you with godly jealousy, for I have espoused you to one husband, that I may present you as a chaste virgin to Christ. But I fear, lest by any means, as the serpent beguiled Eve through his subtlety, so your minds should be corrupted from the simplicity that is in Christ.

For if he that cometh preacheth another Jesus whom we have not preached, or if ye receive another spirit, which ye have not received, or another gospel, which ye have not accepted, ye might well bear with him. (2 Corin 11:2-4)

— And so, it is written, the first man Adam was made a living soul, the last Adam was made a quickening spirit. Howbeit that was not first which is spiritual, but that which is natural, and afterward that which is spiritual. The first man is of the earth, earthy, the second man is the Lord from heaven. (1 Corin 15:45-47)

In his letters to the Corinthians, he stated that, he has espoused them (the Christian) to one husband whose name is Jesus. He continued by telling them that he is afraid that as the Serpent (the Devil) through his subtlety deceived Eve, so he may turn their minds from the simplicity that is in Christ by turning them unto another Jesus. Apostle Paul was sharing his revelation about how the devil deceived Eve the wife of Adam in the Garden of Eden, to the Church of Jesus Christ which he has purchased with his own blood. He went further to explain to the Church their position with Jesus Christ by telling them that he has espoused them to one husband who is Jesus. Just like Eve, the wife of Adam was deceived in the Garden of Eden; the

Old Serpent entered the Church right from the beginning of the Church to continue his deception, by deceiving the Church who is the wife of the second Adam (Jesus Christ), this time with the preaching of another Jesus, another spirit and another gospel.

Paul the Apostle has made the matter clear to us, so that we can see and know the deceivers through their teachings and preaching about Jesus Christ. He referred to such deceivers as the preachers of another Jesus and another gospel with another spirit.

The Jesus whom Apostle Paul introduced to the Church is the Lord God from heaven, and the purpose of His coming is to save a fallen man from eternal destruction. When Adam and Eve sinned against God in the Garden of Eden, it was their spirit that died so they were disconnected from their God. So, when Jesus Christ (the second Adam) came to restore life to man's spirit, He had to die physically in the position of man, so that He could give life to man spiritually. Eve, the wife of Adam in the Garden of Eden was taken from the rib of Adam. The Church, the wife of the second Adam was taken from the rib of the second Adam on the cross of Calvary when they pieced the sword through His ribs. That is why the Bible calls Jesus the last Adam and the life giving Spirit. Apostle Paul by the revelation given unto him has made the Church of Jesus Christ to know that, the devil will send people into the Church to seduce the Church with the preaching of another Jesus.

To resist the deceit of these deceivers, we must know the Jesus whom the Apostles preached to the Church and the work He came to do here on earth. We must also be fully acquainted with how He finished His work and whom He handed the continuation of His work unto. We must know where He is and His promise unto His children (the saints). In these last days of hardship, many people think the best way to make money is to set up a Church in the name of Jesus where they will be preaching the people into their pockets, with their own enticing messages of the people's expectation and not God's expectation.

— Now I beseech you, brethren, mark them which cause divisions and offences contrary to the doctrine which ye have learned; and avoid them. For they that are such serve not our Lord Jesus Christ, but their own belly; and by good words and fair

speeches deceive the hearts of the simple. Rom 16:17-18. This is the main reason why repentance and holiness is being replaced by the preaching's of miracles, blessings and so on.

This can be compared to the scriptures that said in the last days seven women would hold unto a man to just put his name upon them, and they will eat their own food and put on their own clothes. The true Christians (the children of Jesus) are in Christ and Christ Jesus is in us through the baptism of water in the Name of Jesus Christ and the baptism of the Holy Spirit in Jesus' name. And the food given to His Church is the Apostles' *DOCTRINE*, and so Jesus told Peter three times that if you love me feed my sheep with the apostolic doctrine. As Gentile converts let's see how the Apostle whom the Lord Jesus Christ Himself chose for us introduced Him to His Church.

1) Apostle Paul preached that Jesus Christ (the Messiah) came into this world to save sinners. (*1 Timothy 1:15*)
2) Apostle Paul preached Jesus Christ the Lord from heaven (*1 Corin 15:47*)
3) Apostle Paul preached Jesus Christ the Son of God (*Acts. 9:20*)
4) Apostle Paul preached Jesus Christ, the God who manifested Himself in the flesh, and said that is the Pillar and the ground of the true Church of the living God. (*1 Timothy 3:15-16*)
5) Apostle Paul preached Jesus Christ, the Rock who followed the Israelites from Egypt to the Promise Land. (*1 Corin.10:2-4*)
6) Apostle Paul preached Jesus Christ, the Spirit that dwells in the saints, His children as the Holy Spirit. (*Col.1:26-27, Gal. 2:20, Gal.4:4-7*)
7) Apostle Paul preached Jesus Christ the Savior in whose name the sinners are to be born again through water and spiritual baptism. (*Acts 19:1-7*)
8) Apostle Paul preached Jesus, the CHRIST. (*Acts 9:22*)
9) Apostle Paul preached Jesus Christ, the coming Lord who is coming for His Church. (*1 Thess.4:13-18*)
10) Apostle Paul preached Jesus Christ the One who will crown His saints on that day. *(2 Tim.4:8)*

Anyone who preaches and teaches Jesus Christ as the second Person in the trinity is preaching and teaching idolatry because he is preaching another Jesus whom the disciples did not preach. The Jesus whom His disciples preached is the Lord from heaven who arrested Saul (Paul) on his way to Damascus to persecute His disciples for preaching Him whom the Jews have rejected as their Lord. But after He arrested Saul, he began to preach Jesus the Lord and was persecuted by the same Jews for proclaiming Him, as their Lord. Daniel saw Him as the Son of God when He revealed to him what is going to happen in the last days but told him to seal it up because it was not yet time for that revelation. To reveal what He told Daniel to seal, He revealed Himself to Apostle John as the First and the Last, the Alpha and Omega the beginning and the end, also the Lion of the tribe of Judah. So let's see from the scriptures what Apostle John has to say about Him.

— And when I saw him, I fell at his feet as dead. And he laid his right hand upon me, saying unto me, Fear not, I am the first and the last: I am he that liveth, and was dead, and behold I am alive for evermore, Amen: and have the keys of hell and of death. Write the things which thou hast seen, and the things which are, and the things which shall be hereafter: The mystery of the seven stars which thou sawest in my right hand, and the seven golden candlesticks. The seven stars are the angels of the seven churches: and the seven candlesticks which thou sawest are the seven churches. (Rev 1:17-20)

The book of Revelation has silenced every unnecessary argument about the identity of Jesus Christ, and so if you have been called to preach Him to the world you must know Him and don't preach Him wrongly to His children because we are going to give an account for whatever teaching or preaching we make about Him to His children, may the Lord bless you as you search the scriptures.

CHAPTER EIGHT

PREACHING ANOTHER JESUS, ANOTHER SPIRIT AND ANOTHER GOSPEL

— For if he that cometh preached another Jesus, whom we have not preached, or if ye receive another spirit, which ye have not received, or another gospel, which ye have not accepted, ye might well bear with him. (2 Corin 11:4)

— And Jesus answered and said unto them, take heed that no man deceive you. For many shall come in my name, saying, I am Christ and shall deceive many.

Then if any man shall say unto you, lo here is Christ, or there, believe it not. For there shall arise false Christs, and false prophets, and shall show great signs and wonders, insomuch that if it were possible, they shall deceive the very elect. Behold, I have told you before. (Matt 24:4-5, 23-25)

And I saw three unclean spirits like frogs come out of the mouth of the dragon, and out of the mouth of the beast, and out of the mouth of the false prophet. For they are the spirits of devils, working miracles, which go forth unto the kings of the earth and of the whole world, to gather them to the battle of that great day of God Almighty. Behold, I come as a thief. Blessed is he that watcheth, and keepeth his garment, lest he walk naked, and they see his shame. (Rev 16:13-15)

Our Lord and Savior Jesus Christ, has given the needed instruction for the church's awareness, not to be deceived. He said many shall come in His name saying they are the Christ, and shall deceive many.

The Lord has already shown unto His church the ways and means the false Christ shall deceive many. He said they shall show great signs and wonders, insomuch that, if it were possible, they shall deceive the very elect, and ended by saying *"I have told you before"*. Please get the understanding and stop arguing with those who are without understanding. There is a very big difference between the called out (many) and the few chosen ones (the elect.) That is why Apostle Paul told Timothy his son in the Lord to avoid foolish and unlearned questions which engender strife. Every word that Jesus spoke must come to pass. He has given us the understanding when he said *"many are called but few are chosen"*. So, if he said the false Christ and the false prophets shall deceive many by their miracles, signs and wonders then he has already given the understanding unto the elect (the chosen ones) not to follow any so called man of God because of their signs and wonders, or miracles. This is the meaning of Apostle Paul's statement of *"For if he that cometh preach another Jesus, whom we have not preached, or if ye receive another spirit, which ye have not received, or another gospel"* because it takes Jesus and the Spirit of Jesus Christ to preach the gospel. So, for Satan to deceive the people of God he needs to present unto them another Jesus and another spirit so that they can preach another gospel which the true disciples did not preach, this is where the confusion enters Christianity. *I release the apostolic light to shine now in your heart to understand the TRUTH about Christianity in the name of Jesus Christ our Lord and Savior. Amen!!!*

Apostle Paul wrote, about another Jesus, another spirit and another gospel, to the Church in Corinth who were in Christ Jesus but were being troubled by some preachers of another Jesus with another spirit and another gospel, to make them understand that these people are not from God. So he told them that Satan disguises himself as an angel of light to deceive the children of light, thus it is not surprising that his ministers also transform themselves as the ministers of light so that they can deceive the children of light. Please understanding this, anybody who preaches and teaches Jesus Christ as a separate person from the Father, is preaching and teaching another Jesus. Anybody who preaches and teaches the Spirit of God or the Holy Ghost as a separate spirit from Jesus Christ is preaching and teaching another spirit. Anybody who preaches and teaches the death, burial, and the resurrection of Jesus Christ and will not conclude that He was the Father who passed through this process of death, burial and resurrection to save the fallen man who was dead and buried in sin is preaching and teaching another gospel. As a matter of fact, if persecution can let you know the Truth, Apostle Paul should have been preaching the Truth before he met the Lord Jesus Christ on his way to Damascus. Let's see what Jesus told Philip, one of His disciples when he asked Him to show them the Father and that one alone would be enough for them.

— Philip saith unto him, Lord, show us the Father, and it sufficeth us. Jesus saith unto him, have I been so long time with you, and yet hast thou not know me, Philip? He that hath seem me hath seen the Father, and how sayest thou then, show us the Father? Believest thou, not that I am in the Father, and the Father in me? The words that I speak unto you I speak not of myself, but the Father that dwelleth in me, he doeth the work. Believe me that I am in the Father, and the Father in me, or else believe me for the very works sake. --- Even the Spirit of truth whom the world cannot receive, because it seeth him not, neither knoweth him, but ye know him, for he dwelleth with you, and shall be in you, I will not leave you comfortless, I will come to you. Yet a little while, and the world seeth me no more, but ye see me, because I live, ye shall live also. At that day ye shall know that I am in my Father, and ye in me and I in you. (John 14:8-11, 17-20)

— There is one body, and one Spirit, even as ye are called in one hope of your calling. One Lord, one faith, one baptism, one God and Father of all who is above all, and through all and in you all. (Eph 4:4-6)

— And when I saw him, I fell at his feet as dead. And he laid his right hand upon me, saying unto me, Fear not, I am the first and the last. I am he that liveth, and was dead, and, behold, I am alive for evermore, Amen, and have the keys of hell and of death. (Rev 1:17-18)

If we read faithfully the above scriptures and ask for God's mercy to understand His Word, we will conclude that there is no Trinity but One God who manifested Himself in the flesh for the salvation of man-the sons and daughters of Adam.

Jesus is the husband to His own Church, and the Father to the children born into the Church. He is the Spirit which dwells in His true Church as the Holy Ghost. In fact, there are so many things about Jesus Christ which if He was to reveal unto His children who are flesh and blood, we would not be able to contain. When the Apostle John saw Him, even though he was in the spirit, yet he fell before Him as a dead man until Jesus put His right hand on him just like how He protected Moses. If one can understand Jesus as the husband of His own Church, the Father of His own children and the Holy Ghost, who dwells in His children, it will help remove the veil of Trinity from his mind, and help him to understand Jesus who was revealed in the book of Revelation as the Lamb of God who came to take the sins of this world away, and at the same time the Lion of the tribe of Judah who dwells in His children, protecting them. He is the One who paid the price to save sinners and at the same time the One who will judge sinners. He is the Lord and the Lord's Christ, the Savior who died for the sin of man, the children of the first Adam in the Garden of Eden. After salvation he entered His glory as the Father receiving the worship of His children, the sons and daughters of the second Adam born again into the Church, the spiritual Garden of Eden.

CHAPTER NINE

THE GOOD WINE AND THE WINE OF THE WOMAN'S FORNICATION

If you have humbly and faithfully followed this book, then at this point you are in the valley of decision. You are either saying in your heart should I accept the TRUTH (the Good Wine) or should I continue with the doctrine of Trinity (the Wine of the Woman's Fornication). If you are a Pastor or a teacher of God's Word, you may be thinking of the many things you have told your congregation and have even proven to them from the Bible, but now the same scriptures are proving you wrong because of the understanding you have now got from the Bible through the explanation in this book. Read the following scriptures for more understanding; *When the ruler of the feast had tasted the water that was made wine, and knew not whence it was (but the servants which drew the water knew) the governor of the feat called the bridegroom, and saith unto him, every man at the beginning doth set forth good wine, and when men have well drunk, then that which is worse, but thou hast kept the good wine until now. This beginning of miracles did Jesus in Cana of Galilee, and manifested forth his glory, and his disciples believed on him. (John 2:9-11)*

The Bible recorded the first miracle Jesus did was in Cana at a marriage feast, when the people have already been served with the worse wine, but when Jesus and his disciples went to the place of the feast the taste of the wine changed from worse to good, and the governor of the feast called the bridegroom and said unto him *"every man at the beginning doth set forth good wine, and when men have well drunk, then that which is worse, but thou hast kept the good wine until now"*. The governor of the feast did not know the source of the good wine which was new in their taste, but the old wine; however the servants knew where the new wine came from. The disciples who were chosen by Jesus Christ were given a doctrine (wine) to distribute to the elect and declare the Lordship of our Lord and Savior Jesus Christ to his chosen people, who shall be saved through the acceptance of Him as their Lord and Savior and baptism in His name, Jesus. This is the simplicity of the Apostolic doctrine (The Good Wine) which the Apostles were persecuted for, and not by unbelievers, but by the people of God (the Jews) who rejected the new thing (the distribution of the New Wine) that the Lord was doing, and calling it heresy by beating and killing many with the motive of stopping the flow and distributing of the New Wine (the Apostolic Doctrine). Since every word that came out from the mouth of Jesus Christ must come to pass, they fulfilled the Word of Jesus Christ which He said; people will kill you thinking they are doing the work of God (God's service). Please take note of what Jesus said about the sower, "The sower sowed the WORD but when men slept the enemy came in and sown" The disciples sowed JESUS, but when they died (slept) the devil came in and sowed the doctrine of God the Father, God the Son and God the Holy Spirit. The Lord who knows all things has said "this gospel shall be preached to the whole world and the end shall come. The first miracle the Lord did at the Marriage Feast in Cana has now become the last Miracle He is doing through the surface of the earth just before our wedding (the rapture). This is where many great men of God who have preached Trinity will exclaim ***"Oh God, thou hast kept the good wine until now".***

    Who can tell today, how many people have been killed through religious wars? Many religions believe that "the best way I can please my god is to kill you, if you don't believe the same thing with me". The question behind this heartless act is this; if the god you are pleasing is the One who created man in His own image, according to the Christian belief, will He be happy with you if you kill a human being who He created in His own image? And this killing legislated by religious beliefs is going to increase and get worse as a sign that the Rapture is very near. Believe it or not it is coming sooner, very soon, so prepare for it. If we understand the picture of the prophetic ladder which our Lord and Savior Jesus Christ drew down for His followers (the Church). We will seek strength in His Spirit, so that we can withstand the things that are coming upon man on this earth, as it is revealed in the scriptures. Let's read the following scriptures for the confirmation.

— All these are the beginning of sorrows. Then shall they deliver you up to be afflicted, and shall kill you, and ye shall be hated of all nations for my name's sake. And then shall many be offended, and shall betray one another, and shall hate one another. And many false prophets shall arise and shall deceive many. And because iniquity shall abound, the love of many shall wax cold. But he that shall endue unto the end, the same shall be saved. (Matt 24:8-13)

— Because thou hast kept the word of my patience, I also will keep thee from the hour of temptation, which shall come upon all the world, to try them that dwell upon the earth. (Rev 3:10)

— And when he had opened the fifth seal, I saw under the altar the souls of them that were slain for the word of God, and for the testimony which they held. And they cried with a loud voice, saying how long, O Lord, holy and true, dost thou not judge and avenge our blood on them that dwell on the earth? And white robes were given unto every one of them, and it was said unto them, that they should rest yet for a little season, until their fellow servants also and their brethren, that should be killed as they were, should be fulfilled. (Rev 6:9-11)

It is written that "Heaven and earth shall pass away but my words shall not pass away". Every spoken word of Jesus Christ must come to pass or to its fulfillment. The Lord said the first shall be last and the last shall be first. If the Koreans, Africans and the Chinese who have just come to Christ, are preaching Jesus Christ, the Lord of Lords, and the Americans who have been in the field for many years and claim that they are our leaders in Christianity are still preaching God the Father, God the Son, God the Holy Ghost (trinity) which originated from Rome and not Jerusalem, then it is a fulfillment that, the first shall be the last and the last shall be the first. The good wine of the Apostolic doctrine is simply teaching and baptizing converts in Jesus' name for the remission of sins and declaring the Lordship of JESUS CHRIST over all. That was what the disciples of Jesus Christ were persecuted for, by their own people including Paul.

— And when they had brought them, they set them before the council, and the high priest asked them, saying, did not we straightly command you that ye should not teach in this name? And, behold, ye have filled Jerusalem with your doctrine, and intend to bring this man's blood upon us. And they departed from the presence

of the council, rejoicing that they were counted worthy to suffer shame for his name. and daily in the temple, and in every house, they ceased not to teach and preach Jesus Christ. (Acts 5:27-28, 41-42)

The above scripture is enough to confirm to you that the Good Wine that Jesus provided at the Marriage Feast is symbolic to the apostolic doctrine with He, Himself being the source, while His disciples serve it. The Lord Jesus knew how the devil could use the city of Rome against His true Church. Acts chapter 10 has the story of the Italian, Cornelius, a centurion whom the Lord saved with his people who were serving in the military in Caesarea, but that alone was not sufficient for God to deal with a rebellious Rome, so He revealed Himself unto Apostle Paul by night in other to send him to Rome to go and testify unto them about Jesus so that if any DOCTRINE arises from there, you and I can trace it out from the scriptures, and that is why we can now trace the Wine of the Woman's fornication. Let's see from the scriptures what God told Apostle Paul.

— And the night following the Lord stood by him, and said, Be of good cheer, Paul, for as thou hast testified of me in Jerusalem, so must thou bear witness also at Rome. (Acts 23:11)

If we study the Apostle's letter to the Romans from the chapter one, we would understand the great city that the Bible talks about in the Book of Revelation. If we receive the Truth about God's Word we are helping ourselves, but if we reject God's Word with our imagination, God will leave us to imagine and do our own things which will lead us to destruction. Jesus said, this message of the kingdom shall be preached in the whole world and the end shall come. This means no matter how the devil and his demons will try to cover the TRUTH about the kingdom's message (heavenly Gospel); God will still make a way that the whole world would hear, for a testimony against it. So if men refuse to preach it, as the disciples preached and were killed, God will send angels to preach the **GOSPEL.**

— And I saw another angel fly in the midst of heaven, having the everlasting gospel to preach unto them that dwell on the earth, and to every nation, and kindred, and tongue, and people. saying with a loud voice, fear God, and give glory to him, for the hour of his judgment is come, and worship him that made heaven, and earth, and the sea, and the fountains of waters. (Rev 14:6-7)

Apostle Paul explained to the Church of God who was at the city of Corinth that, the gospel is the death, the burial and the resurrection of Jesus Christ. That was exactly what he was persecuting the Church of Jesus Christ (the Apostles or disciples) for. And as it is written that "I will have mercy upon whom I will have mercy), God's mercy found Apostle Paul among the persecuting team who were on their way to Damascus to arrest the disciples and deliver them to be imprisoned for preaching a blasphemous doctrine, because they were declaring the Lordship of Jesus Christ over the Jewish nation which had already rejected Jesus because of the blindness that had come upon them. When God by His mercy called Paul into the ministry, he preached exactly what he persecuted the Church for. When the TRUTH was revealed to Paul, the very group among his persecution team turned against him, persecuting him from city to city. They even arrested him and handed him to the Gentiles for the fulfillment of God's Word. Let us see what Paul said about the preaching of the Gospel.

— *According to the glorious gospel of the blessed God, which was committed to my trust. And I thank Christ Jesus our Lord, who hath enabled me, for that he counted me faithful, putting me into the ministry, who was before a blasphemer, and a persecutor, and injurious, but I obtained mercy, because I did it ignorantly in unbelief. (1 Tim 1:11-13)*

— *Be not thou therefore ashamed of the testimony of our Lord, nor of me his prisoner, but be thou partaker of the afflictions of the gospel according to the power of God. Who hath saved us, and called us with an holy calling, not according to our works, but according to his own purpose and grace, which was given us in Christ Jesus before the world began, but is now made manifest by the appearing of our Savior Jesus Christ, who hath abolished death, and hath brought life and immortality to light through the gospel, whereunto I am appointed a preacher, and an Apostle, and a teacher of the Gentiles. (2 Tim 1:8-11)*

Apostle Paul, who was saved from persecution and made a preacher-man by the Lord Jesus Christ, preached Jesus Christ in his first sermon in Damascus that, **"he is the Christ, the Son of God".** The Apostle continued to grow in the Lord from revelation to revelation into maturity as he could then see the Lord, and hear from Him directly, so he discovered that Jesus was not only the Son of God but the God who came in the flesh to die for man's salvation. The early fathers of the Christian faith (the Apostles) did not preach or teach "Trinity" God the Father, God the Son, God the Holy Ghost. They taught and preached Jesus the Lord from the revelation they received from Him. Apostle Paul clarified it for us when he said, "the last Adam was the Lord from heaven" and told his son in the Lord, Timothy, that godliness is a great mystery, that the God (Jehovah) of their fathers was manifested in the Flesh.

According to the book of Revelation 14:6, John said he saw an angel with the everlasting Gospel preaching unto them that dwell on the earth, telling them to fear God and give glory to Him, for the hour of His judgment is come, and worship Him that made heaven and earth, and the sea, and the fountains of waters. The Bible does not contradict itself, it speaks plainly that Jesus Christ created all things and that alone qualified Him as the One true God who deserves our worship, who also we call our Father who art in heaven. That is why we are born again in his NAME through the baptism of water and of the Spirit as kingdom citizens. Immediately after the proclamation of the true God whom we must worship as Christians another angel followed, saying "Babylon is fallen, is fallen, that great city, because she made all nations drink of the wine of the wrath of her fornication".

After that another angel with a loud voice said *"if any man worship the beast and his image, and receive his mark in his forehead, or in his hand the same shall drink of the wine of the wrath of God"*. As Gentiles our teacher and Apostle, Paul has already got the revelation about that Great City who changed the **TRUTH** of God into a lie and has tried to deceive the whole world with her doctrine. Let's read the scriptures and compare them and see if we have drunk the Wine (Doctrine) of the Woman's Fornication, so that we can come out of the Woman as God has warned His people to come out from her, and not be part of her punishment.

— Because that, when they knew God, they glorified him not as God, neither were thankful, but became vain in their imaginations, and their foolish heart was darkened. Professing themselves to be wise, they became fools. And changed the glory of the incorruptible God into an image made like to corruptible man, and to birds, and four-footed beasts, and creeping things. Wherefore God also gave them up to uncleanness through the lust of their own hearts, to dishonor their own bodies between themselves. Who changed the truth of God into a lie, and

worshipped and served the creature more than the Creator, who is blessed forever. Amen! (Rom 1:21-25)

— So he carried me away in the spirit into the wilderness, and I saw a woman sit upon a scarlet colored beast. Full of names of blasphemy, having seven heads and ten horns. And the woman was arrayed in purple and scarlet color, and decked with gold and precious stones and pearls, having a golden cap in her hand full of abominations and filthiness of her fornication. And upon her forehead was a name written, MYSTERY, BABYLON THE GREAT, THE MOTHER OF HARLOTS AND ABOMINATIONS OF THE EARTH. And I saw the woman drunken with the blood of the martyrs of Jesus. And when I saw her, I wondered with great admiration. -- And the woman which thou sawest is that great city, which reigneth over the kings of the earth. (Rev 17:3-6, 18)

If we read carefully the Book of the Prophet Isaiah from the chapter 14 the verse 12-15 and consider very well, Satan's statement he made by saying–*"he would sit at the mount of the congregation and be like the most high",* it will help us to understand the Book of Romans chapter one and the purpose of that Great City that deceives the nations of the world with the Wine of her Fornication (God in Three Persons Blessed TRINITY) which John saw in the Island of Patmos, and is written down for the Church in the book of Revelation. As a matter of fact, if you are part of the preachers and teachers of God's WORD who preach and teach God in Three Persons, you are sharing the WINE of the WOMAN'S fornication to the people of God. Because the mystery of the WINE of the Woman's fornication is nothing other than preaching and teaching the One True God and the Lord of the Jews as THREE PERSONS (blessed Trinity). That is the mystery (the WINE of her fornication) of the cup in the hand of the Woman, in the 17th chapter of the Book of Revelation. If none of the Apostles of Jesus Christ preached and taught God in Three Persons and baptized their converts in the Name of the Father and of the Son and of the Holy Ghost, which are mere titles Then why are you doing that because the Romans started it, then what do you think you are giving to God's people?

To the Jews there is One Lord, and One God, who revealed himself unto Moses, and sent him to go and deliver His people from the hands of Pharaoh and the Egyptians and lead them to the promise land. The greatest commandment given to the Jews is to acknowledge that their God is one Lord, which they were commanded to know, love with all their heart, mind, might and their strength, and love their neighbor as themselves.

This was the last test they gave unto Jesus when they saw His knowledge which they couldn't withstand. The Bible said God is a rewarder of those who diligently seek Him. Just as if Jesus Christ hadn't gone to the cross, there wouldn't have been salvation, so it is, the book of Acts would have been a story or a history book without the four Gospels because, as the cross carried Jesus up for our salvation, so the four Gospels carried the book of Acts because the commandment that gave birth to the book of Acts was conceived in the four gospels. That is why careful studies of the book of John will give you the understanding that Jesus Christ is the God of the Jews who promised to visit them. And if God promised to visit His children who are flesh and blood how will He come to them? Please I am not talking about the out pouring of the Holy Ghost, remember He first came into them in the flesh before telling them to wait for Him to go back into His glory before He would sent the Holy Ghost into them (born of the Spirit) because it takes Spirit to give birth to spirits. This is the confirmation of what God said in the Garden of Eden after the fall of Adam. So if John saw an angel of God having the everlasting gospel to preach unto the people of this earth it is not another **GOSPEL** but the same **GOSPEL** which the Apostles preached.

When the Lord entered into Jerusalem sitting on a colt, there were praises of Hosanna, Hosanna and the Pharisees ordered Him to tell His followers to stop but turning unto them He said if they hold their peace, the stones will immediately start praising Him, which means if man will not praise Him the stones will do it. But we should remember that stones were for the punishment of certain sins in the Bible. So, if the men of God who are called would not preach the apostolic gospel, angels from heaven will be commanded to preach it unto men. After doing what men have been called to do what would these angel do unto men if God allowed them? Because they have already said *"what is man that God is so concern about"*. To be a believer and a preacher of the everlasting gospel which John saw an angel preach unto the people on this earth, let us see from the following scriptures how the early apostolic fathers, Apostles Paul and John, recorded it down for us to follow.

— Neither can they prove the things whereof they now accuse me. But this I confess unto thee, that after the way which they call heresy, so worship I the God of

my fathers, believing all things which are written in the law and in the prophets. (Acts 24:13-14)

— Therefore, when they were come hither, without any delay on the morrow I sat on the judgment seat, and commanded the man to be brought forth. Against whom when the accusers stood up, they brought none accusation of such things as I supposed. But has certain question against him of their own superstition, and of one Jesus, which was dead, whom Paul affirmed to be alive. (Acts 25:17-19)

— And when I saw him, I fell at his feet as dead. And he laid his right hand upon me, saying unto me; fear not, I am the first and the last. I am he that liveth, and was dead, and behold, I am alive for evermore. Amen, and have the keys of hell and of death. (Rev 1:17-18)

If one becomes a disciple, his or her argument is based on the knowledge of whose disciple he or she is. Any man of God who reads the book of John and the book of Revelation and compare them to Paul's letters to the churches and doesn't know that the One True God of the Jews and the Christians is Jesus Christ, is deceiving himself and the followers that God has called him to. In Christianity today, many so-called men of God are using faith in Jesus' name and are getting the result with God's Word but not with the knowledge (revelation) of who Jesus is. Many people are called men of God because of the miracles they do, and this is where many children of God are being deceived. Since name is for identification, Moses asked God that, if I go and the people (the Hebrews) ask me what is the Name of the God that has sent you, what shall I tell them? When Jesus Christ called His disciples He showed to them the NAME of the God who is sending them. When Apostle Paul was called into the ministry, God showed him, His NAME which is not different from what Jesus told His disciples. This book is to help you break away from religion to Christianity, but the choice is left to you to think about it. The testimony of Paul was all about JESUS CHRIST of Nazareth, Jehovah of the Jews and the God of Abraham who came in the form of man to save the world.

CHAPTER TEN

THERE ARE THREE THAT BEAR RECORD IN HEAVEN AND ON EARTH.

--- For there are three that bear record in heaven, the Father, the Word, and the Holy Ghost, and these three are one. And there are three that bear witness in earth, the spirit, and the water, and the blood; and these three agree in one. If we receive the witness of men, the witness of God is greater, for this is the witness of God which he hath testified of his Son. He that believeth on the Son of God hath the witness in himself, he that believeth not God hath made him a liar, because he believeth not the record that God gave of his Son. And this is the record, that God hath given to us eternal life, and this life is in his Son. He that hath the Son hath life, and he that hath not the Son of God hath not life. These things have I written unto you that believe on the name of the Son of God, that ye may know that ye have eternal life, and that ye may believe on the name of the Son of God. (1 John 5:7-13)

Among the twelve Apostles of Jesus Christ everyone was given a particular revelation to write down for the Church of God to understand and follow, and this is done by the selfsame Spirit of God known as the Holy Spirit, that is why Jesus said, now the true worshipers shall worship the Father in truth and in Spirit because it is the Spirit that searched the deep things of God. Because God is a SPIRIT, before man who is created in His own image can fellowship with Him in Spirit and truth after the fall of Adam and Eve, the dead spirit of man needs resurrection from death before he can hear and understand him, that is why He has given to us (His saints) his Spirit the Holy Ghost. God is a Spirit, and since He is the same Spirit that moved men to write the Bible, there is no contradiction in His WORD, therefore if we see contradictions and confusions it either comes from man's interpretation of God's word with his canal understanding or the devil's quotation in stand to deceive men, but yet we are without excuse, if we follow his lies.

If we compare the witness of John the Baptist about Jesus Christ to the revelation that God gave to His servant Apostle Paul, we will not be confusing ourselves, unless we want to. The above scriptures are to be studied very well and in understanding them lies the victory over the devil's deceit of the belief of the TRINITY which originated from Rome and not Jerusalem. Apostle Paul made the matter clear for us through the revelations he received from the LORD JESUS CHRIST during his ministry, and has recorded them down for our benefit. The responsibility lies with us to study his letters to the Churches with humility and prayer and not with argument. In his letters to the Corinthians, he stated that *"All things are of God, who hath reconciled us to himself by Jesus Christ, and hath given to us (the Apostles) the ministry of reconciliation. To witness that God (who is a Spirit) was in Christ (The Son who was flesh and blood) reconciling the whole world unto himself, and not imputing their trespasses unto them, and hath committed unto us (His Apostles) the WORD of reconciliation".*

Due to the abundant revelation God gave to the Apostle Paul, he revealed everything the Lord wants us to know as His children, so he said *"The Lord is that Spirit and where the Spirit of the Lord is, there is liberty".* So if we follow humbly our teacher and Apostle Paul, we will land upon the foundation of the Jewish faith of **"HEAR OH ISRAEL THE LORD OUR GOD IS ONE LORD"**

Thus, the religious belief of God in THREE PERSONS, BLESSED TRINITY is not part of the Apostolic witness given about JESUS CHRIST as the ONE TRUE GOD of the Jews who manifested in the flesh. Therefore, confirming the belief of TRINITY with 1 John 5:7-13 and other scriptures is a diversion from the CHRISTIAN FAITH because what makes a Christian victorious is the FAITH he or she has in that God who is a SPIRIT has manifested Himself in the flesh through CHRIST by coming to save his children who are flesh and blood. If there is any SAVIOR in heaven apart from the CREATOR, then he will take all the glory and the worship from the Creator and this is exactly what the true Christians are doing in giving the worship and the praise unto Jesus Christ the Son of God. But glory be to God, that He revealed Himself in the book of Revelation as the one who lived, died and resurrected who is ALIVE forever more.

So the three that bear record in Heaven and on Earth is not a proof of TRINITY, but an explanation that God who is the Father came in the form of a fallen man, whom He created in His own image, to die in his stead in giving the gift of the NEWBIRTH unto him, that is why Jesus Christ is known as the second Adam, the Lord God from Heaven. Apostle Paul made it clear to the Church that, the WORD he preached was to bring man back to God who is the Father, and the record of the Holy Ghost is receiving the Holy Ghost which is Christ in me the hope of glory with the evidence of speaking in tongues and for the confirmation as a child of God so that you can call God (Jesus Christ) your Father. The Bible does not teach three separate Gods, neither one God in three persons, but One God, who is the Father of all creation and SAVIOR of a fallen man whom He created for His worship. He is the Holy Ghost (Christ in me the hope of glory) who dwells in His people for regeneration.

Many preachers with their carnal mind preach and teach that the Son who is Jesus Christ is standing at the RIGTHT HAND OF GOD and is interceding for the saints but the Bible says it is the Holy Ghost which dwells in the saints that intercedes in them, so let us search the answer from the following scriptures and be blessed.

---Likewise the Spirit also helped our infirmities, for we know not what we should pray for as we ought, but the Spirit itself maketh intercession for us with groaning which cannot be uttered. And he that searcheth the hearts knoweth what is the mind of the Spirit, because he maketh intercession for the saints according to the will of God. (Rom 8:26-27)

---In the beginning God created the heaven and the earth. And the earth was without form, and void; and darkness was upon the face of the deep. And the Spirit of God moved upon the face of the waters. And God said, let there be light, and there was light. (Gen 1:1-3)

--- In the beginning was the Word, and the Word was with God, and the Word was God. The same was in the beginning with God. All things were made by him, and without him was not anything made that was made. In him was life, and the life was the light of men. And the light shineth in darkness, and the darkness comprehended it not. (1John 1:1-5)

---I am the Lord, and there is none else, there is no God beside me, I girded thee, though thou hast not known me. That they may know from the rising of the sun, and from the west, that there is none beside me. I am the Lord, and there is none else. I form the light, and create darkness, I make peace and create evil. I the Lord do all these things. (Is 45:5-7)

CHAPTER ELEVEN

THE SPIRIT OF TRUTH AND THE SPIRIT OF ERROR

– BELOVED, BELIEVE, not every spirit, but try the spirits whether they are of God: because many false prophets are gone out into the world. Hereby know ye the Spirit of God: Every spirit that confesseth that Jesus Christ is come in the flesh is of God: And every spirit that confesseth not that Jesus Christ is come in the flesh is not of God: and this is that spirit of antichrist, whereof ye have heard that it should come; and even now already is it in the world. Ye are of God, little children, and have overcome them: because greater is he that is in you, than he that is in the world. They are of the world: therefore, speak they of the world, and the world heareth them. We are of God: he that knoweth God heareth us; he that is not of God heareth not us. Hereby know we the spirit of truth, and the spirit of error. (1 John 4:1-6)

The Lord God and the Father of the Christian faith whose name is Jesus has given us Christians the needed road map to our destination by choice to Heaven or Hell. He took His time and taught His Church the signs that lead one into heaven or hell. The Lord did not teach His followers the way and the lifestyle of heaven only but taught also the way and the lifestyle of hell and placed man in the position of choice. The struggle for souls to heaven or hell is the main problem here on earth so Apostle Paul made the matter clear to us by saying *"we are not fighting with flesh and blood but with the spirits that our eyes cannot see"*. That is the plain truth about what is going on in this planet earth where mankind dwells. We should not forget that in the Garden of Eden where God placed man, He gave him His word and gave man the choice to obey or disobey.

The reason one cannot force another to do the will of God is the gift of choice that God himself planted in man after creation, so no one can take that gift from man. That is why man can willingly end in Heaven or hell by his choice and be there to enjoy or to weep forever and ever. The two opposing spirits that are searching for souls to their final destination or kingdom are Jesus Christ and Satan. The Bible describes Jesus as the Lord God from Heaven, and Satan as the god of this world, whose final destination is the lake of fire with his children and his demons the fallen angels. The written word of God is not written for writing sake, but to save man from the everlasting lake of fire. The Lord Jesus Christ doesn't want His people to be misled by any false spirit so he has given to His Church any needed revelation through His Spirit to help His children to be delivered from the hands of the deceivers, so He put a difference between Himself and the devil by calling Satan the god of this world. Remember the witches and wizards are to Satan and his demons what the saints are to Jesus Christ that is why the Bible says, "suffer not a witch to live".

The difference is very clear because of what these two spirits have to offer. The God of Heaven is calling His people unto Himself through the heavenly things and the god of this world is also pulling people down with the worldly things, and so the Lord said we shall know them by their fruits. That does not mean as Christians we should be poor, lacking the worldly things before we can qualify to live for the Lord, or be able to take part in the rapture. Everything for man's enjoyment was given unto Adam before the fall. The Apostle John admonished the Christians not to believe every spirit, but try them whether they are from God, because many false prophets have gone out into the world. The scriptures wrote that Prophets are the vessels of spirits, either the TRUE SPIRIT known as the Spirit of God, the Holy Spirit or the Spirit of Christ, and the spirit of the devil and the demons known as false spirits, who in other to deceive the children of God (Jesus Christ) disguise themselves as the Spirit of God.

The Apostles already taught us how to know these false spirits and the Spirit of God by saying every spirit that confesses that Jesus Christ has come in the flesh is of God. No matter how the men of God today demonstrate their anointing and power through miracles and wonders, the difference is clear. If they don't preach and teach like the Apostles of old, then they are portraying to the Church a false spirit, the Bible says by their fruits you shall know them. Jesus Christ the Son of God and the son of

David asked the Pharisees about the CHRIST, whose son is he? He concluded by asking them if he is the son of David, how then did David in the spirit called Him Lord?

While the Pharisees were gathered together, Jesus asked them, saying, what think ye of Christ? Whose son is he? They say unto him, the son of David. He saith unto them, how then doth David in spirit call him Lord, saying. The Lord said unto my Lord, sit thou on my right hand, till I make thine enemies thy footstool? If David then call him Lord, how is he his son? And no man was able to answer him a word, neither durst any man from that day forth ask him any more questions. (Matt 22:41-46)

Our Lord Jesus Christ told His disciples that, unto them it is given to understand the mysteries of the Kingdom, but unto others it is not given so it shall be in parables. For one to understand that Jesus was the Son of God on earth and the Lord in Heaven at the same time is the greatest mystery of the Christian faith. This is what Apostle Paul saw and said "great is the mystery of godliness, that God who is a Spirit was manifested in the flesh" it takes the Spirit of Christ who dwells in the Prophets of old and God's Prophets of today to know Jesus Christ is the Son of God revealed in the flesh and the same time the Lord God in heaven, the Lion of the tribe of Judah and at the same time the Lamb of God. In 1st Peter the chapter one, Peter explained that He was the Spirit of Christ that dwelt in the Prophets of old, that will help us to know the spirit of the antichrist or the spirit of error through their teachings about Jesus Christ.

Now get the understanding, right from Genesis to Revelation the Spirit of Christ testifies about **ONE TRUE GOD** who created all things alone and promised to come and save a fallen man, because if there is any Savior apart from the Creator, then who takes the glory of our salvation? So the Bible says – *Yet I am the Lord thy God from the land of Egypt, and thou shalt know no god but me; for there is no savior beside me. (Hosea 13:4.)* This is what God did through Jesus Christ our Lord and was testified unto us who want to be part of the kingdom's citizenship. The Apostles who were chosen as witnesses, witnessed Jesus Christ the Lord God and the Savior of the world, to His chosen children. If the chosen servants of Jesus Christ testified about Him as the Lord God from heaven then who created the doctrine of trinity if not the spirit of error or the antichrist? Because the Spirit of Christ-God in His servants testified about ONE GOD to His people, that has been the sign of the true Spirit of Christ-God from Geneses to Revelation.

Woe to the rebellious children, saith the LORD, that take counsel, but not of me; and that cover with a covering, but not of my spirit, that they may add sin to sin: That walk to go down into Egypt, and have not asked at my mouth; to strengthen themselves in the strength of Pharaoh, and to trust in the shadow of Egypt! Therefore shall the strength of Pharaoh be your shame, and the trust in the shadow of Egypt your confusion. (Is 30:1-3)

It all started from the Garden of Eden after the sin of Adam and Eve. When they saw their nakedness after their disobedience, they covered themselves with fig leaves. God did not leave them with their own COVERING but shed blood of an animal to make a covering for them since they were still His own image on earth. God puts difference between His chosen people (by covering them with His Spirit) and those who deceives themselves that they are for Him but are not but only use His name for miracles. Because many miracle conscious ministers of the gospel have ended up in Egypt-the kingdom of darkness taking their strength and power from Pharaoh-the devil for miracles in the name of the Lord Jesus Christ by deceiving their followers. So the Bible says:

And I saw three unclean spirits like frogs come out of the mouth of the dragon, and out of the mouth of the beast, and of the mouth of the false prophet. For they are the spirit of devils, working miracles, which go forth unto the kings of the earth and of the whole world, to gather them to the battle of that great day of God Almighty. (Rev 16:13-14)

WHY DID THE LORD PROMISE TO POUR HIS SPIRIT UPON MAN?

— And it shall come to pass afterward, that I will pour out my spirit upon all flesh; and your sons and your daughters shall prophesy, your old men shall dream dreams, your young men shall see visions: And also upon the servants and upon the handmaids in those days will I pour out my spirit. (Joel 2:28-29)

The Bible has the answer to whatever we want to know in our relationship with God if we can search the scriptures. After the fall of Adam and Eve, they fell short of the glory of God, and found themselves naked. They died spiritually but were still living souls and the images of God who lived in the flesh. For the Lord God, the Creator to save man-the sons of Adam and Eve, He put on flesh (He became like man-the image of God) so that He could deliver man in his three natures, body, soul and spirit. He poured His soul (blood) to deliver man's soul from sin. He poured His Spirit upon the spirit of man to give the dead spirit of man spiritual life, as the Bible says the spirit of man is the candle of the Lord. So the Spirit of Christ is in the Church to continue the work of Christ until the rapture. The GREAT COMMISSION is to go into the whole world and preach salvation unto the dying world and allow the Lord to do the miracles according to His own will. The disciples of Jesus Christ preached the GOSPEL, the death, the burial and the resurrection of Jesus Christ as the foundation of TRUTH and baptized their converts in Jesus' name for the remission of sins. Jesus said I came that you would have life and have it more abundantly. So if the Spirit of Christ which He poured into His Church is at work in the Church and in the world, wouldn't the Church continue His work in giving the light of salvation to His people? The suffering of Jesus Christ on the cross of Calvary is not for personal gain, it is for the soul saving of the people, so the true Spirit of Christ is still at work which is SALVATION, in preaching repentance and the remission of sins unto this dying world.

HOW THE HOLY GHOST WORKS IN THE CHURCH

1) The Holy Spirit in the Church is still calling sinners to "come and let us reason together, if your sins be like crimson it shall be as white as snow" and so the operation of the Holy Ghost in the Church and in the world is to call sinners unto repentance before the evil day comes.

2) The Holy Ghost (the Spirit of Christ) empowers the Church to deliver the children of God from destruction, through the preaching of the GOSPEL of Jesus Christ.

3) The Holy Ghost (the Spirit of Christ) is given unto the Church to teach the doctrine of Christ known as the Apostolic doctrine so as to deliver the saints from any false doctrines especially the DOCTRINE OF DEVILS as stated by Apostle Paul in the book of Timothy who Jesus Christ called purposely for us the Gentiles who were idol worshippers.

4) The Holy Ghost (The Spirit of Christ) is given to the Church to empower her to fulfill God's calling amid persecution.

5) The Holy Ghost (The Spirit of Christ) is poured into man's dead spirit to give life to his spirit so that he can be connected to Him and worship Him in TRUTH and in SPIRIT, as the Bible says God is a Spirit because it is the Spirit of God in man's spirit that makes man to understand the voice of God and live for Him, as it is written the Spirit searches the deep things of God.

6) The Bible says those who have not the Spirit of Christ (the Holy Ghost) are none of His. So, the Holy Ghost is purposely for adoption as a child of Jesus Christ that is why it is written that Christ in us is the hope of glory.

7) The Holy Ghost does not force people to worship God whether they like it or not but convince them by warning man to run away from the dangers ahead.

9) The Holy Ghost (the Spirit of Christ) is given to help the children of God to know the spirit of the antichrist so as not to be deceived. In order not to be deceive by any other spirit, it is written that: ***The Lord-Jesus is that Spirit, where the Spirit of the Lord-Jesus is, there is liberty.***

10) Finally, the Holy Ghost is given to the Christians to empower them to overcome any spirit that will arise to fight against them in this evil world, because this world is a battle field where man is fighting with the spirits which his eyes cannot see.

CHAPTER TWELVE

THE MYSTERY OF THE RAPTURE AND THE RESURRECTION

Now this I say, brethren, that flesh and blood cannot inherit the kingdom of God; neither doth corruption inherit incorruption. Behold, I show you a mystery; We shall not all sleep, but we shall all be changed, In a moment, in the twinkling of an eye, at the last trump: for the trumpet shall sound, and the dead shall be raised incorruptible, and we shall be changed. For this corruptible must put on incorruption, and this mortal must put on immortality.

So, when this corruptible shall have put on incorruption, and this mortal shall have put on immortality, then shall be brought to pass the saying that is written, Death is swallowed up in victory. O death, where is thy sting? O grave, where is thy victory? The sting of death is sin; and the strength of sin is the law. But thanks be to God, which giveth us the victory through our Lord Jesus Christ. Therefore, my beloved brethren, be ye steadfast, unmovable, always abounding in the work of the Lord, forasmuch as ye know that your labour is not in vain in the Lord. (1 Corin 15:50-58)

Apostle Paul has made the matter clear for the true Christians in saying there is a hope for those who are suffering persecution for their faith. He said, if it is in this world only that we have hope as Christians then we are more miserable than anybody else. Any preacher or a teacher of the gospel who denies the rapture and the resurrection of the dead, is not working for the Lord Jesus Christ but for the antichrist. They are treading the old path of the deceivers who existed during the days of our Lord Jesus Christ and his apostles. Some false teachers have referred to the out pouring of the Holy Ghost on the day of Pentecost as the second coming of the Lord, making their followers to believe that the Lord has already come. There are lots of beliefs that are contrary to the teachings of the Apostles of Jesus Christ.

In Christianity, what one believes is not what matters, but what Jesus and his disciples taught the church that it is going to happen. During the days of Jesus Christ and his Apostles, they faced challenges from people who were believers but denied that there is resurrection of the dead (life after death.) Whether they believed or not, Jesus explained to them that there is going to be the resurrection of the dead for both the good and the evil from where man is going to be judged finally from where he would spend eternity in heaven or in the lake of fire, to fulfill the word of God that says *"it is appointed for a man once to die after that judgment".*

Many people have the belief that what they affirm is the only Truth or what God is going to do at last, for that simple reason they reject every other Truth so far as it is not what they were taught without searching the scriptures, no matter who taught it. The Apostles of old did not allow what they heard from their opposers to change their message of salvation to mankind. For the doctrine of the resurrection, Jesus Christ said —*Marvel not at this; for the hour is coming, in the which all that are in the graves shall hear his voice. And shall come forth: they that have done good, unto the resurrection of life; and they that have done evil, unto the resurrection of damnation. (John 5:28-29)*

Frankly, something very important is missing from today's apostolic message, specifically, the message of the rapture, the Lord's return for His Church in the sky. This is the reason why many ministers of God's word are telling the devil, to give them the whole world and take their souls and the souls of their followers. The reason why many are fed up with the doctrine of the rapture or the catch away of the saints, is that, many took to themselves and predicted the coming of the Lord Jesus Christ which never came to pass, so people don't want to be deceived any more by those who teach prophecy wrongly and put the children of God in the state of confusion.

When Jesus was speaking about His second coming which is purposely for His children, He did not give us a specific date or hour but taught about the signs that will precede His coming. Apostle Paul also wrote to his son in the Lord, Timothy about the signs of the last days. Due to how people interpret the scriptures, many people, Christians and none Christians alike are thinking that the world is going to end at the coming of the Lord Jesus Christ. The last days that the Bible talks about is not the end of the world but the end of this dispensation of grace or Church age, because when the Church is taken to glory people are going to stay in this evil world and pay the price for rejecting the gospel which was for their salvation. No matter how the teachings of the rapture is getting covered in the Church today, the Spirit of the Lord is still active in the children of God to help them understand the time and be prepared for the Lord's return, just like the sons of Issachar who knew the time. To encourage the discouraged brethren in Thessalonica, Apostle Paul wrote to them about the mystery of the rapture which is the hope of every child of God.

— *But I would not have you to be ignorant, brethren, concerning them which are asleep, that ye sorrow not, even as others which have no hope. For if we believe that Jesus died and rose again, even so them also which sleep in Jesus will God bring with him. For this we say unto you by the word of the Lord, that we which are alive and remain unto the coming of the Lord shall not prevent them which are asleep. For the Lord himself shall descend from heaven with a shout, with the voice of the archangel, and with the trump of God: and the dead in Christ shall rise first: Then we which are alive and remain shall be caught up together with them in the clouds, to meet the Lord in the air, and so shall we ever be with the Lord. Wherefore comfort one another with these words. (1 Thess 4:13-18)*

The reason why many Christians are living the Christian life carelessly is because they joined Christianity just for what God can do for them and not what they can do for God. Somebody asked a question that if God is the One who created everything, then what can we give Him to please Him? The answer is so simple, because it is written that God is not willing that a soul should perish, so to please Him we must give back our whole being (body, soul and spirit) unto Him by obeying His WORD for our salvation and not stay in the Church deceiving ourselves. It is written that when a sinner repents from his sins there is joy in heaven, why? Because the angels of God see that person running from the anger of God into His saving hands. My friend, the RAPTURE is real, and it is coming sooner than you think whether you believe it or not. Likewise there is going to be resurrection for every human being to be judged, this is what Jesus said in John 5:28-29. Please read the following scriptures for more understanding and look for the true Church of Jesus Christ where salvation is being preached without fearing that the people will leave the Church.

—And the devil that deceived them was cast into the lake of fire and brimstone, where the beast and the false prophet are, and shall be tormented day and night for ever and ever. And I saw a great white throne, and him that sat on it, from whose face the earth and the heaven fled away; and there was found no place for them. And I saw the dead, small and great, stand before God; and the books were opened: and another book was opened, which is the book of life: and the dead were judged out of those things which were written in the books, according to their works.

And the sea gave up the dead which were in it; and death and hell delivered up the dead which were in them: and they were judged every man according to their works. And death and hell were cast into the lake of fire. This is the second death. And whosoever was not found written in the book of life was cast into the lake of fire. (Rev 20:10-15)

CHAPTER THIRTEEN

FAITHFULLNESS IN STEWARDSHIP

— Let a man so account of us, as of the ministers of Christ, and stewards of the mysteries of God. Moreover, it is required in stewards, that a man be found faithful. (1 Corin4:1-2)

— Fear none of those things which thou shall suffer; behold, the devil shall cast some of you into prison, that ye may be tried; and ye shall have tribulation ten days; be thou faithful unto death, and I will give thee a crown of life. He that hath an ear let him hear what the Spirit saith unto the churches; He that overcomes shall not be hurt of the second death. (Rev 2:10-11)

Our Lord and Savior Jesus Christ asked Apostle Peter; three consecutive times, do you love me more than these? And Peter answered yes; and the Lord said feed my sheep. Before the Lord handed over the keys to the kingdom of God unto Apostle Peter, He first tested him trice to see how faithful he would be in the kingdom's stewardship. Peter as his occupation was had faced challenges in struggling with his boat, the net, great fishes and storms as fisherman in the sea, but Jesus called him into a ministry of fishing for men. Although he was an old experience fisherman, but that did not qualify him for his new ministry and assignment, so the Lord tested him to see how faithful he would be if he faced challenges with men in the world and not fishes in the sea. Let's see from the scriptures how Peter was prepared from one stage to another, before his new ministry. **Luke 5:1-10** has the story.

From the pages of the scriptures we see that Jesus first sat in Peter's boat and started preaching to the multitude. After coming out from the boat he told Peter to get into the boat with his people, move forward a little and thrust his net into the deep. Peter explained how they had tried all night without catching any fish, so he told Jesus that *"by thy WORD we shall throw the net"* due to obedience they threw the net and caught the greatest number of fishes ever in their occupation, and that led to Peter's confession of *"depart from me I am a sinner".*

After Peter's confession Jesus told him "Fear not, from henceforth thou shall catch men", as a matter of fact CONFESSION is the key to enter into God's mercy and compassion, and so the Bible says if we confess our sins unto the Lord He is faithful and just to forgive us our sins. *1 John 1:8-10*

Because of the nature of God's work He doesn't put people into His ministry anyhow; He calls and trains His people (vessels) from one stage to another before He puts them into the ministry. Now let's trace from the scriptures how Peter was prepared from one stage to another until he became the one whom Jesus gave the keys of the kingdom to. The Bible tells clearly that at the Lake of Gennesaret, people pressed on Jesus to hear the WORD of God, so he saw a ship that belong to Peter and entered the ship and commanded him to move away a little from the Land, and Peter obeyed. So He sat in the ship and started preaching the word to the people.

Peter's first preparation was that he gave his vessel with obedience unto the Lord to use. After passing the first test he needed another test when the Lord told him to now enter into the ship for a catch. With his humanly experience he saw the impossibility of catching any fish at that time, but he said by your WORD we shall throw the net. After throwing the net and catching many fishes, he confessed his sins by telling the Lord to depart from him for he is a sinner, because He came to save sinners; He told Peter that "from henceforth you shall catch men". By obedience from one stage to another the Bible says they forsook all and followed Jesus, Peter and his companion in the boat, when they saw the miracle that Jesus did.

The Lord trained Peter from one stage to another, but he did not qualify to handle the keys of the kingdom until he reached the REVELATION stage. At the miracle stage when he caught multitude of fishes, Peter confessed Jesus, the Lord knowing that to the Jews, (the descendants of Abraham) they have one Lord and one God. But at the REVELATION stage he confessed Jesus, the Christ, and the Son of the living God. It was that same revelation John the beloved received when he wrote that God has given us life and the life is in His Son (the Christ).

Many have jumped into the ministry through the windows and not through the door of preparation from step to step where a man is tested at every step that is why there are lots of confusions and many falling into destruction, because they don't know where they belong to in ministry. About seven of the disciples of the Lord were fishermen, who knew how to catch fish, but needed to be trained on how to catch men. In fishing the fisherman needs first a boat, second a net, and must know how to swim, because it is a dangerous business, as the fishes are caught in the sea, rivers or Lakes, one can drown if he doesn`t know how to swim. Just like at the Lake of Gennesaret where Jesus sat in Peter's ship and preached to the multitude, the Lord always needs a vessel to dwell in through His Spirit called the Holy Spirit to preach to the people and save them.

Now get the understanding, every fisherman must have time to work on his boat seasonally and amend his net. Man is the boat of God in whom He dwells as the Holy Spirit to catch men in the Sea which is the world. So as a servant of God you are the boat, the sea is the world, the net is the word of God, the fishes are men. Due to the dangers and deception by the devil and his ministers, men of God need to be trained in every stage in ministry so that they can fulfill God's calling in their lives. For every man of God to be able to accomplish his given duty in the Lord he must understand his calling and operate within the circle of that calling because the Bible says if you break the hedge a serpent will bite you. One doesn't need to be like Elijah or Elisha to fulfill his calling in the Lord. Many who wanted to be like the other ministers had fallen into the water, just like the borrowed axe in the book of second Kings Chapter six. Apostle Paul made this clear unto the church by saying ***"measuring themselves with themselves they are not wise"***.

Many people today claim the call of God on their lives but have no message. It is a fact that one can be called into the Church for salvation but must wait to be prepared for a mission in God's ministry so as to know what he has been called to do. When Apostle Paul heard God's calling on his way to Damascus, he asked that ***"what wilt thou have me to do?*** And the Lord told him to arise and go into the city and it shall be told him what he must do. Then, God sent Ananias to go to him and lay his hands on him and prayed for him to receive his sight and his ministry.

Today many people boast of titles and degrees they have achieved from Bible colleges, but when we talk about Kingdom messages, they have no substance. Jesus told the people of his time, that **"now the true worshippers shall worship the Lord in Truth and in Spirit, because God is a Spirit and must be worshipped in Truth and in Spirit"**. I have heard people say that Peter did not go to school, These are the thoughts Satan uses to putting somebody on the seat of illiteracy. These people forget that Jesus called the disciples and taught them to go, teach and preach to the world.

It takes a student to become a teacher that is why people who refused to learn from another do not develop in anything. Bible college is so important in these our days but one thing a man of God needs to understand is that your main ministry from God is what you have been called to do. The purpose of the Bible college is to give you some needed understanding on how to go about your ministry and how to deal with people out of people's experience especially from the examples of the people of old in the Bible. As a matter of fact the best Bible teacher for your Bible College is God's chosen pastors at whose feet you sit daily and hear from, out of their experience, as the Bible says "it happened unto them for our example and it is written down for our learning.If someone is called into the ministry and has at least five genuine men of God whose feet he sits while they share their experience with him, that person will be better than someone who has graduated from these Bible colleges. The reason is simple as this; most of these Bible colleges are for the antichrist, so people go to those Bible colleges to learn the mind of Satan through his chosen servants. Staying under the feet of the Lord and receiving from Him is spiritual but how to give the spiritual food to the carnal people is also another thing. That is why one must know how to apply both laws, spiritual and carnal. Apostle Paul made that mistake in Corinth. So he said I have given you strong meat or bones instead of milk. Now let us draw a conclusion from this.

The Lord Jesus asked Peter, three times that do you love me more than these? And based on Peter's positive response he told him to feed his sheep. And so any steward in the ministry of God has some special food from the Lord to give unto His sheep (children.) It is left for us to face facts and ask ourselves if we are called to minister by God. Am I giving to the people the kingdom's message? Am I faithfully serving between the Lord and His people or do I copy people's yesterday's messages (food) and give to the people of God today?

As servants of Christ and the stewards of the mysteries of God, if we can faithfully serve in His kingdom we must know what is given unto us to serve his children with. Apostle Paul used his son in the Lord Timothy as a role model for us to follow, and so let's hear from his warning to Timothy some of his important mysteries which he commanded him to hold fast to and to teach his followers. This would help truly decipher if we are genuinely also part of these faithful stewards of mysteries or are deceiving ourselves. — *Likewise must the deacons be grave, not double tongues, not given to much wine, not greedy of filthy lucre; Holding the mystery of the faith in a pure conscience. And let these also first be proved; then let them use the office of a deacon, being found blameless. (1 Tim 3:8-10)*

—*These things write I unto thee, hoping to come unto thee shortly. But if I tarry long, that thou mayest know how thou oughtest to behave thyself in the house of God, which is the church of the living God the pillar and grand of the truth. And without controversy great is the mystery of godliness. God was manifest in the flesh, justified in the Spirit, seen of angels, preached unto the Gentiles believed on in the world, received up into glory. (1 Tim 3:14-16)*

— *Consider what I say; and the Lord give thee understanding in all things. Remember that Jesus Christ of the seed of David was raised from the dead according to my gospel. Wherein I suffer trouble, as an evildoer, even unto bands; but the word of God is not bound. Therefore, I endure all things for the elect's sakes, that they may also obtain the salvation which is in Christ Jesus with eternal glory. It is a faithful saying; for if we be dead with him, we shall also live with him. If we suffer we shall also reign with him; if we deny him, he also will deny us. If we believe not, yet he abideth faithful; he cannot deny himself. (2 Tim 2:7-13)*

— *O Timothy, keep that which is committed to thy trust, avoiding profane and vain babblings, and oppositions of science falsely so called. Which some professing have erred concerning the faith. Grace be with thee. Amen. (1 Tim 6:20-21)*

A lot of revelation was given to Apostle Paul to write down for the teaching of the church to distinguish from the other churches that are not on the true track to heaven although they confess so. But the foundation on which every other mystery is built upon, is that revelation he received during his calling, which he termed the MYSTERY OF GODLINESS. In this mystery, Apostle Paul said, God was manifested in the flesh through the lineage of King David in the person of Jesus Christ. This is the foundation of every mystery in the Bible for a fallen man's salvation after the fall of Adam and Eve in the Garden of Eden. That is why this selfsame MYSTERY covers the whole Bible from Genesis to Revelation, because without it all the other mysteries would be meaningless.

As stewards of the mysteries of God we don't have the same dishes to serve the children of God within the church else there wouldn't be different gifts in operation for the building of the people of God. As Apostle Paul said we know in part. God has never chosen anybody here on Earth and made him Alpha and Omega. We could see that Moses needed Aaron in the beginning of his calling and during his calling he needed Aaron and Hur who held his two hands for victory for the people of God. Before he ended his mission he needed somebody to continue from where he ended so God provided for him Joshua.

We have been called into the ministry to minister the mind of God unto the people of God in each area of their needs because one can't do all, we need each other's ministry as the servants of God. Where the revelation of your God given mystery ends is where somebody's ministry starts, so if you refuse to move with him, you will end up scratching your dry ground with your carnal imaginations calling them revelation from God. This is one of the greatest mistakes most of the men of God are doing by keeping the children of God in the prison of ignorance. They refuse them from hearing any message from another source, or read Christian books. This is one of the reasons why there is so much dryness in the ministry, although there are many self appointed ministers who are not connected unto the Lord who are confused and confuse their followers, but if the church (the saints) of God are not connected to each other as a body there will be a lot of short-circuiting flow of God's anointing and this may cause the people to walk in one way revelation.

Apostle Paul wrote to his son in the Lord, Timothy that it is a great mystery that God manifested Himself in the flesh, died, was buried and rose up again the third day. And that was the main driving force behind his beatings, persecutions and imprisonments. Today, due to the individualism in the church, the Beauty of Christ is no more seen in the church again. If someone is called into the ministry of prosperity, he turns the whole church into a place of prosperity without salvation. If someone is also called into the ministry for salvation, he turns his church unto a place of salvation without blessing. Some also based on blessings without salvation and holiness. Some who have been called into the ministry of deliverance and spiritual warfare spend all their time casting out demons every minute without prosperity so they get fed up with poverty and stay away from church.

The truth about all these things is that every servant of God (Jesus Christ) is afraid of the thief or the wolves in sheep's clothing, so calling another man of God with a different gift to come and minister in one's church, causes fear of losing the members to him. I dare say most men run their own church with the motive of filling their bellies, so the fear of losing his members to another minister of God would drive him to continue to keep them in ignorance so that he can continue to drain them financially. There is nothing the church is facing now that, the apostles have never passed through before, yet they were more than conquerors due to the common faith that joined them together, as the people of God with One Lord, One Spirit, One faith and One baptism.

They knew their Lord Jesus Christ whom they were all working for, in His own Vineyard. And that being the basis of their faith, they were able to accept themselves although they had different gifts in their ministrations. The main thing that joined Apollos the disciple of John the Baptist to the disciples of Jesus Christ is his acceptance of Jesus being the CHRIST. The Bible described Apollos mighty in the scriptures but had knowledge of the scriptures to the baptism of John the Baptist, but due to his humility he was taken to a higher dimension of faith in Christ Jesus by Priscilla and Aquila who heard him preach and knew that he needed to be taken unto the next level in the Christian faith.

Let's see what the Lord Jesus Christ asked the Pharisees after silencing the Sadducees

"What think ye of Christ? Whose Son is he? They say unto him, the Son of David. He saith unto them, how then doth David in spirit call him Lord, saying. The Lord said unto my Lord, sit thou on my right hand till I make thine enemies thy footstool? If David then calls him Lord, how is he his Son? (Matt. 22:42:45.)

The Lord Jesus Christ Himself has given His disciples, the understanding of the

MYSTERY OF GODLINESS that in the Spirit, Jesus Christ is the Lord to those HE was Son to. That is why David's son is David's Lord. In heaven, His spiritual kingdom, Jesus is David's Lord, but visiting His people for salvation which started from Jerusalem, He became David's Son because He was born through the lineage of King David. As King of kings He had to come through the lineage of a King and as the Lion of the tribe of Judah He came through the lineage of Judah.

That is the main reason why God called Abraham and made nations out from him by showing His nature as ONE LORD, ONE GOD to His people. So if the Jews who are the physical children of Abraham believe in one Lord and one God of their fathers then why do the spiritual children of Abraham believe in God in three persons, blessed TRINITY? I can't say much about the sons of Abraham whom Keturah bare unto him, but it is well known that Ishmael whom Hagar bare unto Abraham, also believed in the one true God of his father Abraham (although he was deceived to believe in Baal who disguised himself as the God of Abraham with the name Allah).

In these times of crisis, it is imperative that the stewards of the mysteries of God feed the children of God with the heavenly food faithfully so that we can get the greatest harvest in the kingdom's work because many will come back home just like the prodigal son.

In Christ Jesus there is no crisis because He supplies our needs. There is a very severe wind blowing with the motive of diverting the people of God from their duty especially the true servants of God who serve the heavenly food unto His sheep. This is the time to stand as the body of Christ holding each other's hands in prayers and intercession on behalf of each other and God will give the victory. So, let's stand in our areas of ministrations for the Lord is our captain, as we follow and serve Him faithfully, victory is assured.

THE FEAR OF THE LORD IS THE BEGINNING OF WISDOM

— For that they hated knowledge, and did not choose the fear of the LORD: They would none of my counsel: they despised all my reproof. Therefore shall they eat of the fruit of their own way, and be filled with their own devices.(Pr 1:29-31)

— When wisdom entereth into thine heart, and knowledge is pleasant unto thy soul; Discretion shall preserve thee, understanding shall keep thee. To deliver

thee from the way of the evil man, from the man that speaketh froward things; Who leave the paths of uprightness, to walk in the ways of darkness. (Pr 2:10-13)

— What man is he that feareth the LORD? Him shall he teach in the way that he shall choose. His soul shall dwell at ease; and his seed shall inherit the earth. The secret of the LORD is with them that fear him; and he will show them his covenant. (Ps 25:12-14)

God has a covenant of salvation with man, to bring his soul out from the path of hell which leads into the Lake of Fire and reveal His truth and ways to those who fear Him. Today many people are running a race called the *"Christian race"* throughout the world, and out of misunderstanding create confusions that lead to hatred and separation among themselves while encouraging themselves that they are on the right track. Heaven is not for those who are anointed to show forth the power of God on earth, but for the humble ones who have the fear of the Lord in everything they do. If a man has the fear of God, he attracts the favour and the compassion of God for salvation unto himself, where the Lord will show him the right way to come unto Him and find rest. The saints of today exercise their faith by hardening their hearts in following the Lord that is why many are seriously defending the doctrine of Trinity which never exists.The Bible says: *"the secret things belong to God"* so if a minister of God will walk in Him with fear and truth, He will continue to reveal what others cannot see unto him. This is the main reason why a servant of God must fear Him.

Many ministers of God have been deceived to believe that miracles, signs and wonders are the only seal of approval as God's servant, so they force themselves to do miracles even if they have not been given that grace. Elijah and Elisha did great miracles according to biblical records. These two great Prophets of God were persecuted by idol worshipers-Gentiles. John the Baptist came in the anointing of Elijah to prepare the way of the Lord but did no miracle. Jeremiah came in with the ministry of DELIVERANCE to deliver the people of God who have gone whoring under the queen of heaven and Baal. He did no miracle but did the greatest work among the Prophets of God by delivering the Jews from false worship. He was persecuted by his own people, from the priest, the Prophets and the elders than any of the Prophets. He did not face any challenge from the Pagans and their gods, but from his own nation the Jews-God's people.

Today ninety to ninety-five percent of the ministers of the gospel for the sake of doing miracles, signs and wonders have ended up in occultism. They have joined associations of Pastors who are falsely known as great men of God in the world and because they join themselves together in working for the god of this world they face few or no persecution at all. The world goes after them, so the god of this world work hand in hand with them, but those who are set apart by God in these last days to deliver His people from the hands of the devil and his ministers will suffer persecution from false ministers of the gospel.

The search of power to do miracles, signs and wonders in the Church today is greater than the search of knowledge and the fear of God that is what is leading many men of God into occultism. As Christians, we are commanded to seek first the Kingdom of God and all its righteousness and all the other things shall be added unto us. In running this Christian race, let our eyes and hearts be fixed on the fear of God, let's put away every form of deceit of ourselves and of our fellow brethren.